TOTAL QUALITY MANAGEMENT
A SYSTEM TO IMPLEMENT
Implementing Continuous Improvement.

GANA KIRITHARAN

http://www.gkiri.com

TOTAL QUALITY MANAGEMENT – A SYSTEM TO IMPLEMENT

By Gana Kiritharan

For information E-mail to:- kirithara@yahoo.com

Canadian Cataloguing in Publication Data

Kiritharan, Gana, 1967-
Total quality management : a system to implement :
Implementing continuous improvement

Includes bibliographical references.
ISBN: 1-894727-01-0

  1. Total quality management. I. Title.

HD62.15.K58 2000   **658.4′013**   **C00-901761-5**

First Published by Gana Kiritharan in 2001.
Published by UBSPD**(978-81-7476-421-8)**(New Delhi – India) 2003 – 2013
Republished by Gana Kiritharan 2013.

ISBN:
Paper Back: 978-1-894727-01-3
E-Book: 978-1-894727-03-7
Lulu Print: 978-1-894727-07-5

Published by:-
Gana Kiritharan
PO Box 92296
2900 Warden Ave
Scarborough ON M1W 3Y9
CANADA
http://www.gkiri.com

THIRUKKURAL

It is an honor to dedicating this book to

Philosopher Thiruvaluvar.

"அறனீனும் இன்பமும் ஈனும் திறனறிந்து
தீதின்றி வந்த பொருள்"

அதிகாரம் 76   குறள் 754

"The wealth acquired with a knowledge of proper means and
without foul practice will yield virtue and happiness."
Chapter 76- Kural 754

Thiruvaluvar had written the Thirukkural over 2,000 years ago. In
1330 Kurals, he sets out an ethical code for all areas of social life that
is not based on any specific religious or ethnic identity.

3

FOREWORD

I am very impressed by the information Mr. Kiritharan has gathered and the determination he makes about its application. He is reaching out to help the reader have a clear understanding.

Most of those in management, as well as many quality professionals, view quality as a sort of add-on to activity. Actually it has to become embedded in the daily activities of each area. We manage to deal with financial management and schedule management as an integral portion of every thought. Continuous emphasis is placed on these two at meeting after meeting. Executives can get fired for not taking proper care of them.

Quality, however, is often handed over to the quality department for caretaking. They work at getting certifications for quality programs or winning awards or helping to meet schedule and financial problems. Most companies with quality problems deliver the majority of their product or service on the last week of the month.

Looking at quality as doing what was agreed rather than 'goodness' is a big step in reversing this application custom. Quality has to be built into the fabric of the organization. I think this book is a big step in bringing this about.

Philip B. Crosby
Winter Park, Florida

PREFACE

Increasing market competition, increasing price of raw materials and improvement in information management system by the usage of computers have all led to a search for a better philosophy in the world of management. Total quality management is the final product of this search.

Almost 75 years have passed since TQM principles emerged as a separate discipline in America. During this time lots of books have been written and many consultants have come up, but still we often hear of big companies having to call back products because of complaints about quality. What are the reasons for this ongoing problem? Quality management consultants agree that implementing quality management strategies requires a change in culture, a change that is often difficult to achieve. This change requires a strong commitment, more consultation, training and education. It is unfortunate that traditional management schools are not yet ready to accept that quality management is a separate discipline that requires a separate program. Marketing principles also need to be changed from advertising techniques to customer expectations.

When I was first introduced to this subject I went to a bookstore—bought a couple of books and tried to expand my knowledge. I faced two problems. First, all of them were written in a language that was difficult to understand for a person who had learned English as a second language. Second, they were written in a technical language for executives and middle managers, which make it difficult for a professional from another discipline or a supervisory person to get much use from such books.

This book is an attempt to provide a solution to the above problems. Quality management principles are simplified as much as possible and written in simple English so that everybody can read and understand them. This book will be of use to professionals from non-management disciplines, supervisory people in all fields and students getting introduced to this philosophy.

ACKNOWLEDGEMENTS

Although it was only recently that I decided to write a book on quality management, I had had dreams of writing a book for many years. It remained a dream for many years due to several barriers. Without help from the following people I would not have been able to break down the barriers, and I would like to extend my sincere thanks to all of them.

I would like to thank all of the teachers and friends at the institutions where I studied and worked throughout my life. These are the people who have educated me, modified and molded me into the person that I am today. My special thanks go to the NIIT and SSI of India, through whom I was introduced to Total Quality Management and Relational Databases. My sincere thanks go to Madurika and all other friends who helped me break the language barrier and structured a wonderful work from my unstructured English. I should thank all the authors and publishers of the reference books that I have used here. I do not have the words to thank S. Ganesalingan whose advice and encouragement made this book possible. My sincere thanks go to Philip B. Crosby for his foreword and encouragement towards my work.

I would like to extend my special thanks to UBS Publishers' Distributors for providing me with this unique opportunity to share my knowledge in the form of this book with the rest of the world.

Finally, I should thank all my relatives and friends who stayed with me and helped me through the difficult periods of my personal life.

ACKNOWLEDGEMENT FOR REFERENCE BOOKS

I would like to extend my sincere thanks to all the authors and publishers of reference books that I have used here. I acknowledge following publishers and authors for granting permission to reprint materials from their books.

Crosby, Philip B., *Quality is Free: The Art of Making Quality is Certain*, McGraw-Hill Book Company, New York, Mentor Printing, January 1980.
Crosby, Philip B., *Quality without Tears: The Art of Hassle-Free Management*, McGraw-Hill Book Company, New York, Plume Printing, April 1985.
(Definitions of Quality Tools developed by Philip B. Crosby and material for Sections 7.5, 10.4 and 11.3 are excerpted from above two Books with permission of the McGraw-Hill Companies.)

Martin M. Broadwell, *The Supervisor and On-the-job Training*, Addison-Wesley Publishing Company, USA, 1995. *(Material for Section 10.2 is excerpted from this Book with permission of Perseus Books Publishers, a member of Perseus Books, L.L.C.)*

Smith, Barry J, *How to Be an Effective Trainer*, John Wiley & Sons, Inc, USA, 1987. *(Material for Section 10.3 is excerpted from this Book with permission of John Wiley & Sons, Inc.)*

Blank, Leonard, *Changing Behavior in Individuals, Couples and Groups*, Charles C Thomas Publishers Ltd., USA, 1996. *(Material for Section 11.2.1 is excerpted from this Book with permission of Charles C Thomas, Publisher, Ltd., Springfield, Illinois.)*

CONTENTS

Chapter One

INTRODUCTION

1.1 TOTAL QUALITY MANAGEMENT: PREVENTING DISASTERS

Human civilization has produced major achievements and inventions in many fields during the 20th century. It may be democracy as a form of governance, the control of infectious diseases in the medical field or the electronic transfer of money in banking and much more; but we are still unable to escape from man-made and preventable natural disasters. Until now, we did not know how to escape economic depression or prevent the bankruptcy of well-established companies. Take the service sector for example; over 20 years have passed since the goal of 'Health for all by 2000 AD' was proclaimed in Alma Ata. We have reached the year 2000 and what have we achieved? One study shows that, of the world's 6.8 billion inhabitants,

- 1.5 billion people are living without safe drinking water.
- 2.5 billion people are living without basic sanitation.
- More than 1 million people are without access to primary health care.

The same study warns that the situation may get worse in the future. What went wrong and why does this reality exist despite all our knowledge and control over Nature. Although a lot of human, monetary and material resources are allocated to solve these problems, we are still failing here. It is not the quantity alone that matters, quality is also important. In our business and service

- Are we allowing our customers to define our goals?
- Are we selecting the least costly method of achieving these goals?
- Are we allowing all our employees to participate in planning our work?

No, not always. So we can see that we are failing to develop a quality system to achieve this target.

If *quality* is the problem, we must first define it and then find a solution. Quality gurus have tried to define the quality problem as, "dissatisfaction with the services provided or failure to achieve the expected standard."[1] Our next question will be "what are the sources of quality problems and how do we prevent them?"

The challenge that is facing us is whether we can understand and implement the total quality management concepts to prevent these disasters before they occur. Before entering into a deeper discussion it might be useful to get a brief idea of the history of the total quality management (or TQM as it is more commonly known) and some brief ideas about its concepts.

1.2 HISTORY[3, 4]

One of the earliest forms of quality assurance can be traced back to 221 BC when in China the Chou Dynasty

---

1 Philip B. Crosby, *Quality without Tears*, 1985, Mentor Printing, Reprinted with permission of the McGraw-Hill Companies.

required that physicians pass an exam before entering into practice. But today's TQM concept arose as a separate discipline in the United States around the 1920s. At that time, quality control meant controlling or limiting the number of defective items that are found in the output of an industrial manufacturing process. In this process the defective products were separated from the others. From this idea of simply separating the bad products from the good ones a more effective management philosophy has arisen with a focus on action to prevent a defective product from being created rather than simply screening out a defective product once it has been made. Great scholars such as Shewhart, Deming, Juran, Feigenbaum, Crosby and several others have made contributions in this direction.

Walter A. Shewhart of Bell Telephone Laboratories was the first person to apply the new statistical method to the problem of quality control. In a memorandum prepared on May 16th 1924, Shewhart made the first sketch of a modern 'control chart'. The new technique was subsequently developed in various memoranda and articles. Finally, in 1931 Shewhart published a book on statistical quality control called *Economic Control of Quality of a Manufactured Product*. The book set the pattern for the subsequent application of statistical methods to the process of quality control. Several tools developed by Shewhart were subsequently improved and utilized by another management consultant, Deming, in his 'Statistical Process Controls' system.

William Edward Deming received his doctorate in mathematical physics. He was born in 1900 and after receiving his doctorate in 1928 worked for eleven years as a mathematical physicist at the US Department of Agriculture. During this period he understood the importance of statistics and got a detailed understanding of Shewhart's tools. Deming extended Shewhart's philosophy of gaining control over variability in the manufacturing process. Deming's philosophy can be reduced into two words—'reduce variation'—and he developed his thinking on the subject into what became known as Statistical Process Control, more commonly SPC. During the period 1939–45, the American Bureau of Census and the US weapons greatly benefited from his advice on the technique of sampling and statistical control that led to manifold productivity increases and cost savings.

Despite Deming's initial success, his thoughts were not fully appreciated by American managers after the Second World War. Immediately after the war, American industry was left in a favourable position. The cost of raw materials was low, markets were expanding and there was little international competition. At that time, quantity was more important than quality and management was more concerned with increasing sales than with reducing costs. Western industry believed that this situation would last forever and ignored the quality-based techniques.

While Quality Management techniques were being sidelined in the west, in another part of the world, the methods gained new relevance. The Japanese industrial structure had been completely destroyed in the war and had to be rebuilt from scratch. The military governor of post-war Japan, General Douglas MacArther, invited Deming to act as a consultant to the Japanese industry. The TQM concepts helped in the reconstruction of

Japanese industry for which all raw materials had to be imported.

While Deming was helping Japanese industry, another quality management consultant, Dr. Joseph Juran, rose to prominence in America. Juran had pursued a variety of careers: in engineering, as an industrial executive, government administrator, university professor, corporate director and management consultant. His experience in America was similar to Deming's and he was also invited to Japan in the early 1950s to conduct seminars for top and middle-level executives. His *Quality Control Handbook* in 1951 led him to international fame. This and other books on quality, namely, *Quality Planning and Analysis* and *Management of Quality*, have been translated into 13 languages. Dr. Juran has made the greatest contribution to the management literature of any quality professional. He received over 30 honorary medals including the highest Japanese decoration, the Second Order of the Sacred Treasures, awarded to him by the Emperor of Japan for "the development of quality control in Japan and the facilitation of US and Japanese friendship".

Alongside American professionals, Japanese quality management professionals such as Taguchi and Ishikawa made important contributions in areas such as variability reduction, problem solving, teamwork and defining and satisfying customers' expectations. As a result of all these innovations, Japanese industry began to grow and Japanese firms started to dominate almost every market that they chose to enter.

During the 1970s the American automobile industry was almost crippled by the increased price of petroleum products and the rapid entry of Japanese firms into the market. Only after this did American managers start to understand the importance of total quality management. The concept of TQM as it is used now developed under the teaching and guidance of Feigenbaum, Deming and Juran in American schools.

Another important contributor to the field of TQM is Philip B. Crosby. Before becoming a management consultant he had worked his way up from line inspector to corporate vice president and quality director of ITT. He promoted his 'zero defect' concept in a series of excellent books, *Quality is Free, Quality Without Tears,* and *The Art of Getting Your Own Sweet Way*. Crosby has taught thousands of company executives and helped hundreds of American companies develop quality management systems for themselves. He is the chairman of Philip Crosby Associates and the director of Crosby's Quality College in Winter Park, Florida. Today TQM continues to grow as a predominant management philosophy in the United States and has spread to Europe and other Asian countries such as India and China.

1.3 CONCEPTS IN TQM[4]

TQM emphasizes a number of concepts and different people have tried to arrange the concepts in different ways. Basically TQM is defined as a "commitment to continuous improvement of quality" not just in industry but also totally in society. This idea can be further divided into three basic concepts, they are:

- Customer satisfaction.
- Defect prevention.
- Employee participation.

In order to achieve the above objectives the following steps have to be taken:

1. Focusing on customer expectations.
2. Developing a quality measurement system.
3. Identifying root causes.
4. Developing a communication system.
5. Employee motivation.
6. Training for quality.
7. Process improvement.

We can arrange these concepts and actions in the following figure for easy understanding.

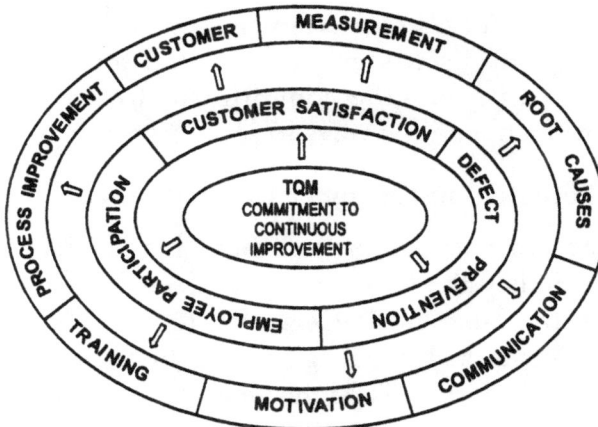

Fig. 1.1 Concepts and Actions in Total Quality Management

Let us have a brief description of these concepts and actions.

1.3.1 Commitment to Continuous Improvement of Quality

It is widely understood and accepted that improvements in the quality of products and services cannot be achieved only by acting for short periods of time or concentrating on a few parts of industry or society. If we need high quality products and services and a good quality environment in which to live, everyone should be prepared to work towards it continuously. Former US President George Bush once said: "The improvement of quality in products and the improvement of quality in services—these are the national priorities as never before."[2] However, years before President Bush asked Americans to work towards quality improvement, Japanese industry and society had started doing just that. TQM is not just the latest management fad, it is a new way of thinking that will require fundamental changes in the way we carry out transactions, not only in business but also in society as a whole. In Chapter Three, I will discuss in greater detail the problems involved in achieving commitment to continuous improvement and the ways to solve them.

1.3.2 Focusing on Customer Expectations

Lee Iacocca once advertised that Chrysler has three rules: "Satisfy the customer, satisfy the customer and satisfy the customer". Certainly for anybody who believes in the quality management philosophy, customer is a golden word. In TQM the word *customer* is defined differently. Instead of the traditional customer outside

---

2. Davis, Elaine R, *Total Quality Management for Home Care*, 1994, Aspen Publishers, Inc.

the company, every transaction, whether it is inside the company or in society is defined as taking place between a service provider and a customer. In Chapter Five, I will explore in detail this way of thinking and other related ideas focusing on customer expectations.

1.3.3 Developing a Quality Measurement System

If we want to improve ourselves we should first identify where we are and what we are moving toward. A good measuring scale would be very useful in this regard. In social sciences such as Economics or Politics, however, finding a measurement scale is not easy. Although money can be used as an index, its mismanagement by government or banks can have disastrous consequences. At the micro level of small companies, the money related index that can be used is profit. Even though it is generally found to be a good measurement index, frequent attempts to make profit on a short-sighted basis can lead to quality disasters. So we try to use indices like Scrap Value and Price of Non Conformance (PONC) to evaluate our productivity. In Chapter Six, we will investigate these indices further and look at other problems related to measurement.

1.3.4 Root Cause Identification

Customer dissatisfaction, falling profit and bankruptcy—all these are symptoms of poor quality. However, the real causes of these problems are usually hidden and difficult to identify. The real cause may be poor techniques, insufficient training or poor management practice. To identify these causes we use techniques and tools like statistical process control, check sheets, brainstorming, fish-bone diagram and pareto charts. In Chapter Seven, I will discuss these tools and the problems in identifying the root causes and how to overcome them.

1.3.5 Developing a Communication System

In order to satisfy the customer, information is required about the customers' likes and dislikes. For this purpose a good communication system must be developed that can give us up-to-date information about customers' expectations. More important is a good communication system inside the company that will record and analyze problems relating to defects and employees' often-valuable ideas on how to solve these problems. The current revolution in information management, made possible by computers, has had made this task easier and more accurate. In Chapter Eight, I will investigate about this and other issues related to communication.

1.3.6 Employee Motivation

Even though quality can be defined by customers and quality objectives by managers, it is the employees who will finally make quality improvements possible. Quality objectives can only be realized when employees are motivated to implement them. So how are we to motivate employees towards quality objectives? The usual management tools such as authority and money will not prove very useful. We need an efficient motivating system and while giving employees share options can help a little, employees will continue to feel alienated as far as they are kept out of the decision-making process. Allowing employees to be involved in the decision-making process is the only way to motivate them to work towards quality improvements. In

Chapter Nine, I will explore the different methods to involve employees in the decision-making process and other issues related to employee motivation.

1.3.7 Training for Quality

Quality management is a newly evolving management philosophy and it is not yet taught in the traditional management schools as a separate discipline. Managers therefore need to be trained in quality management objectives and tools. Employees also need a brief introduction to quality management and its tools in order to dispel fear and ensure efficient participation by all in the new methods. More importantly, however, employees need to be trained so that they have a good understanding of the work that they do and reasons for doing it in any given way. Many of the things we do, not only in our work but also in our day-to-day life are done without an understanding of the reasons for doing them. As a result we cannot make changes in processes that we may not properly understand even if they are causing quality problems. Only a training program that will give employees a real understanding of the reasons behind the processes of their work can help improve quality. In Chapter Ten, I will discuss these training-related issues.

1.3.8 Process Improvement

Collecting information, making measurements and identifying root causes are all important, but nothing changes unless someone does something. The implementation of such strategies will encounter more than a few challenges. People are often resistant to essential change. When planning for long-term gains, the short-term problems, that may or may not be related to the main problem, cannot be ignored. Balancing all these and doing something is an art. It is what management is all about. There is nothing to be scared about it. A good education, intelligence and some experience will teach this to you. In Chapter Eleven, I will discuss the problems related to implementing.

1.4 QUALITY IN INDUSTRY AND QUALITY IN SERVICES

Are there any differences between industry and services in their view of quality management? This is a question that most managers face. What are the basic differences between industry and services? Industry produces goods that are usually countable and prices them according to their market value. But in the service sector, especially in the social services such as government, health and education, constructing a measurement scale to count these services is not easy as the services are not priced through the market mechanism. However, these services are essential to the existence of the market economy. Governments create and implement rules for the operation of the market, educational institutions supply manpower for the market forces and health services help to maintain the productivity of the market's manpower.

Individually elaborating on quality management concepts can help towards understanding the problem with greater clarity. For example, for customer satisfaction, industries are able to modify their products according to customer expectations even though there are some technical standards to follow. In the service sector, however, there is a greater number of standards and regulations. Therefore modifying services according to customers' expectations is often not possible. Changing government regulations, or changing educational syllabi according to the students' expectations is not always feasible. This is not to say that in the service sector nothing can be changed according to customers' expectations. Frequent detailed studies can be conducted to identify customer satisfaction with these services and from time to time modifications can be made. More important than large-scale changes are small changes on the timing or mechanism of service provision that can bring about greater compliance from customers.

In my opinion there is no difference between the services and industry when it comes to defect-prevention. There may be some differences in finding the measurement scales but there will not be significant differences in recording non-conformances and finding the root causes for these problems.

There may be some additional difficulty in implementing employee participation concepts in the service sector. Again knowledge, regulations and standards do not allow modifications in the methods of service provision in accordance with employees' experiences. Perhaps regulations about standards in the service sector do not need to be so strict. Certainly a teacher may know better than an education minister the changes that need to be made with regard to educational standards and would even have some useful information that a PhD in education would not have. So whenever changes need to be made in the service sector, it would be useful to gather the employees' ideas on the matter. In the following chapters, I will discuss the problems related to implementing quality management techniques in the service sector. From Chapter Three to Chapter Eleven, I will try and develop ideas on the relationship between the concepts being discussed and their implementation in the service sector.

With this brief introduction I think it is time to start a detailed analysis of quality management principles. Before the analysis on commitment to continuous improvement in Chapter Three, I will outline in Chapter Two some definitions of terms used in quality management. Definitions are important as quality management is a new management science and there is, therefore, a lot of confusion about the meaning of different terms. In Chapter Four, I will discuss the production process and from Chapter Five to Chapter Eleven, the individual steps that need to be taken for quality management improvement, starting from customers and ending with implementation. In Chapters Twelve, Thirteen and Fourteen, I will discuss some associated knowledge that can help management practices. In Chapter Twelve, I discuss scientific knowledge, in Chapter Thirteen, statistics and in Chapter Fourteen, computers.

Chapter Two

DEFINITION

2.1 DEFINITION OF COMMON TERMS IN TQM

Before defining the terms used in quality management, it is best to try to understand what is meant by *quality*. Asking a class of motivated students for a definition of the terms would provide a number of answers: accountability, availability, price and so on. The choice of the best or most important definition from this group will vary for different people, different situations and different products. Total Quality Management tries to escape this problem by leaving the definition open: 'Customers define quality'. This places a great responsibility on the service-provider, to look beyond education, experience and international standards and towards the customer in order to find out his or her expectations. The problem is not solved even if the customers' expectations are accurately known; changes in situation or simply the passage of time may lead to different expectations. Although the customers' expectations are subject to a great deal of variation, the service-provider is expected to spend time and money in trying to accurately ascertain them. The following four "As" are usually expected from the service-provider by a customer.

1. Accountability
2. Affordability (Price)
3. Availability
4. Appearance.

It is again the customer who decides which of the above is the most important. (This will be discussed in greater detail in Chapter Five.) The term *quality control* used to mean simply screening out defective goods from the production process at the end of the production line. It has now developed into a more sophisticated concept known as *total quality management*, which encompasses methods that aim to prevent the production of defective goods, rather than simply separating them once they have been produced.

Before going on to a definition of total quality management, the term *management* itself must be defined. There are a number of simple definitions, such as 'making decisions', 'getting things done', and so on. A more detailed definition could be:

> Making things and services possible from money, material and human resources by establishing a relationship between these resources and making decisions.

How does the definition of quality management differ from the one given above? Dr. Armand V. Feigenbaum has given a definition for this term:

> Total Quality Management is the agreed company-wide and plant-wide work structure, documented in-effective, integrated technical and managerial procedure, for guiding the coordinated actions of

the people, the machines and the information of the company and plant, in the best and most practical ways to assure customer quality satisfaction and economical cost of quality.

So what is the difference between the traditional definition of management and management processes taken from the quality point of view? Basically both of them accept the importance of resources to the process but Quality Management gives more emphasis to information-oriented co-ordination between these resources. Quality Management also adds the all-important word *'customer'* to the output of the management process. The emphasis in Quality Management is therefore on information in the co-ordination of activities and customer expectations when deciding on the type of product.

2.2 MEASUREMENT TERMS USED IN TQM

The usual measurement scale used in traditional management is money and the desired outcome is profit. Certainly money is a good measuring scale, it can be easily used for both comparison and calculation. What about quality management? Although money is still used, it is not in the form of profit. A number of indices, such as scrap value, COQ, PONC and POC are used for comparison and calculation. Alongside these some other measuring scales are also used. As stated earlier, quality management is about information-orientated administration, and money is not always a useful index for measuring information.

2.2.1 Scrap Value

This is the most immediate and easy quality measurement term that is used. It is obtained by multiplying the amount of scrap produced from the production line by its market value. Even though it is easy to calculate and gives a quick idea of the money that is lost due to the defects that are produced, it fails to give an exact and complete picture of economic losses caused by poor quality. For example, it does not include transportation charges and insurance losses brought about by releasing defective goods into the market. Neither does it take into account the loss in customer satisfaction that is brought about as a result of poor quality. The following terms are used to solve this problem.

2.2.2 Cost of Quality (COQ)

The cost of quality measure gives the amount of money that has to be spent as a result of quality problems within the organisation. Philip B. Crosby, in his book *'Quality is Free'* gives a detailed definition of the measure and ways to calculate it. According to him, it includes:

1. All effects of work over, including clerical work.
2. All scrap.
3. Warranty (including in-plant handling of returns).
4. After-service warranty.
5. Complaint handling.
6. Inspection and test.
7. Other costs of error, such as engineering change notice, purchasing change order, etc.

He develops his ideas on cost of quality further in his book *Quality Without Tears*, where he divides the cost of quality into two parts: price of non-conformance (PONC) and the price of conformance (POC).

2.2.3 Price of Non-Conformance (PONC)

This measure is an expression of the expense involved in doing things wrong at all points in the process. PONC measures the cost involved in correcting sales orders as they arrive, correcting procedures that are drawn up to implement orders and correcting the product or service as it goes along the production line. It also includes the cost of processing warranty and non-conformance claims.

According to Crosby, when all of these different values are added together, the sum will be 20 per cent or more of the value of sales in manufacturing companies and 35 per cent of operating costs in some service companies.[1]

2.2.4 Price of Conformance (POC)

This measure is an expression of the expense necessary to ensure that all products come out right. It includes most of the professional quality functions, all prevention efforts and quality education. The measure also covers such areas as procedural or product qualification. According to Crosby, the cost should come to about 3 or 4 per cent of sales in a well-run company.

---

1. Philip B. Crosby, *Quality without Tears*, 1985, Mentor Printing, reprinted with permission of the McGraw-Hill Companies.

2.2.5 Other Measurement Scales Used in TQM

The above measures are money-orientated quality measures that can be used as management tools by the upper management to understand quality problems. At the department level, however, the number of defects being produced or the types of defects may be better measures as they give a direct understanding of the underlying problems. The type of measurement tool that is preferred will differ from department to department, according to output. When trying to understand defects in the whole company, a few tools should be chosen that would give a good overall picture.

In the service sectors, such as health or government, there are well-developed non-money-orientated measurement scales such as infant mortality and economic growth rate. In Chapter Six, the various scales are discussed in greater detail.

2.3 INDICES USED IN TQM

Alongside the above scales, the following indices are also used in quality management.

2.3.1 Shipped Product Quality Level (SPQL)

This figure measures the number of planned error outputs that are released. The purpose of the measure is to identify the importance or number of service people needed by the company. For example, a manufacturer may intentionally release some computers with defects in order to identify the efficiency of the customer complaints system. All such products should be traced to the customers and should be replaced with new products as soon as the complaint is received.

In the service sector, a patient could be released without a clinical note in order to identify the efficiency of the field midwife, or an artificial problem could be created in the government sector in order to identify administrator's abilities to identify and solve the problem.

2.3.2 Acceptable Quality Level (AQL)

This is a figure of total output, perhaps 1 or 2 per cent that is considered an acceptable figure for the level of defects. It is usually set for supplies and provides an acceptance level for inspection or test personnel.

2.3.3 Zero Defects

Crosby introduced this concept in his series of books; it suggests that attempts to set an acceptable level of defects in the production process, either through AQL or any other measure, will become a threat to the level of quality in the process. The concept suggests that necessary action should be taken to prevent and correct every single mistake in the production line.

2.3.4 DIRFT (Do it Right for the First Time)

According to Crosby DIRFT is the mechanism through which the 'zero defects' ideal can be achieved. It involves ensuring that requirements are clearly understood and giving employees all the necessary tools to meet them.

2.4 TECHNIQUES AND TOOLS USED IN TQM[3]

Several techniques are used in TQM to identify and analyse the defects that occur during the production process and prevent them. A brief explanation of some of the tools is given here; more detailed descriptions will be given during the course of the book, as needed.

2.4.1 Mass Inspection

This involves inspecting every single item that is leaving the factory in order to identify the defects. It is the traditional method of quality control. When a defective item is identified, it is removed and either sent to be repaired or thrown away. It is a time-consuming and costly procedure.

2.4.2 Statistical Quality Control (SQC) or Statistical Process Control (SPC)

This method replaced the traditional mass inspection method. Instead of checking every single item in the output, this method identifies a number of variables along the production line that influence the quality of the end product. These variables are checked either manually or through electronic detectors with the help of a sampling process.

When a variable begins to move out of a prescribed limit, the production process is stopped or brought down to a minimal level. Only after the variable has been brought to the desired level is the production process allowed to resume at normal capacity. The variables that are usually checked are the quality of inputs, environmental factors that may influence the production process and the quality of intermediate products. Although SQC is thought to be a complicated process to implement, actually it is not.

2.4.3 Variable

This is not a specific TQM term; it is a mathematical term. A property of a variable is that, when being measured, it will give different values between people or items. For example, the height of an individual within a population is not fixed and will vary from person to person and the variation is not limited, so height is a variable. In contrast, the number of fingers possessed by individuals within that population is constant; it is fixed at 10 (for individuals without deformities) so it is called *constant*.

Variables in Nature have some specific characteristics, for example if the number of individuals within a population of different height is counted and then a curve of number of individuals against height is plotted, a specific pattern is obtained. In Chapter Thirteen these characteristics are discussed further.

2.4.4 Checksheets

These are used to record variables in the production process. They can be used to ensure that the variables are at the desired level (recording conformance) or to detail the defects that are produced (recording non-conformance). More importantly than conformance and non-conformance, checksheets can also be used to maintain stocks and machinery. In hospitals, check-sheets are used to ensure that the necessary procedures are completed correctly before surgery begins. Figure 2.1 gives an idea of how checksheets can be used.

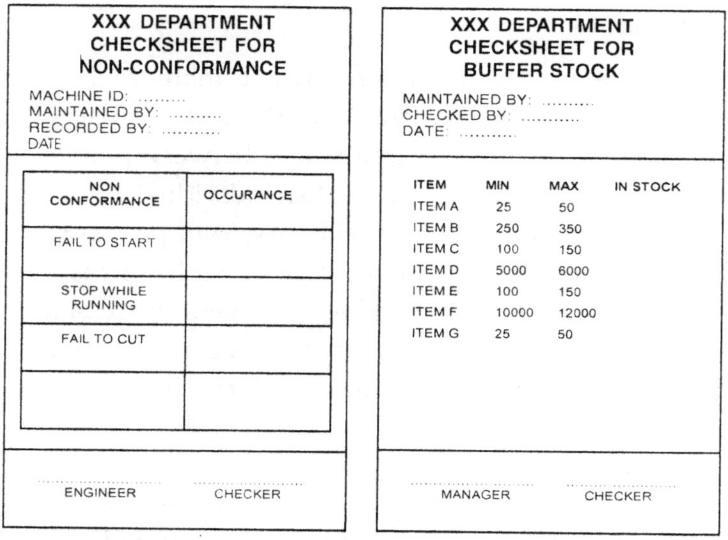

XXX DEPARTMENT CHECKSHEET FOR NON-CONFORMANCE
MACHINE ID: ....
MAINTAINED BY: ....
RECORDED BY: ....
DATE

NON CONFORMANCE	OCCURANCE
FAIL TO START	
STOP WHILE RUNNING	
FAIL TO CUT	

.... ENGINEER   .... CHECKER

XXX DEPARTMENT CHECKSHEET FOR BUFFER STOCK
MAINTAINED BY: ....
CHECKED BY: ....
DATE: ....

ITEM	MIN	MAX	IN STOCK
ITEM A	25	50	
ITEM B	250	350	
ITEM C	100	150	
ITEM D	5000	6000	
ITEM E	100	150	
ITEM F	10000	12000	
ITEM G	25	50	

.... MANAGER   .... CHECKER

Fig 2.1 Checksheets for Non-Conformance and Conformance

2.4.5 Pareto Chart

This chart is used to identify the intensity of each problem in the production line. The type of defects is shown on the horizontal axis and the number of occurrences on the vertical axis. The horizontal axis should show the type of defects in decreasing order of frequency, starting with the most frequent.

2.4.6 Fish Bone Diagram

This diagram is used to identify the relationship between the defects or problems and the root causes underlying them. When finished, the diagram looks like a fish bone, hence the name.

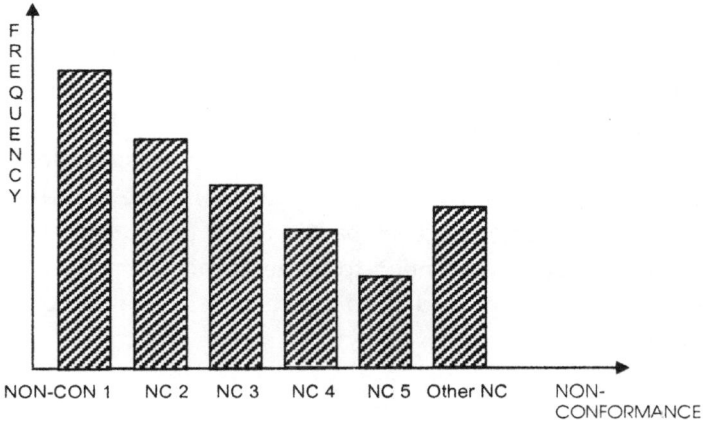

·Fig. 2.2 Pareto Chart

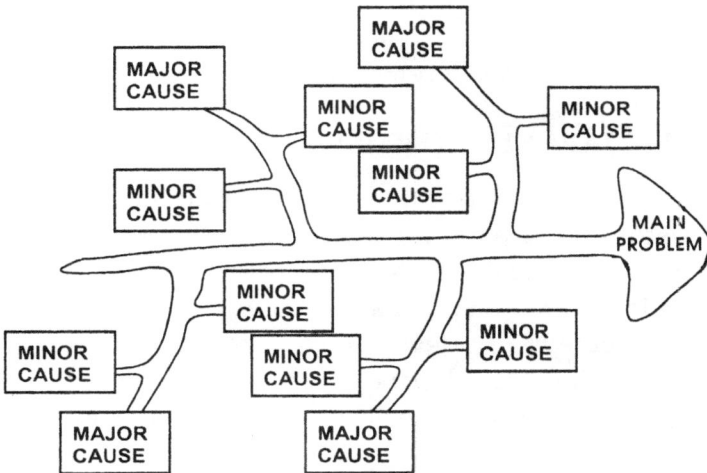

Fig. 2.3 Fish Bone Diagram

2.4.7 Process Definition Flow Chart

When a factory produces a complex product, the production line usually consists of small processes that sequentially add parts to form the final product. In such cases, process charts are drawn, using squares, circles and arrows, to diagrammatically explain the whole process on a single piece of paper. Such diagrams are useful to planners who need to understand the process inside the company and plan corrective action when needed.

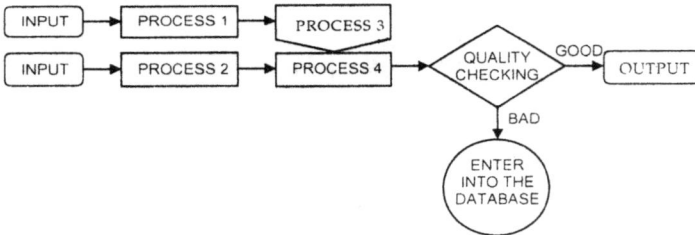

Fig. 2.4 Process Definition Flow Chart

2.5 SOME JAPANESE TERMS[3]

Although many important Quality Management professionals are American, today's quality management systems are tested and modified in Japan. Several Japanese quality management professionals have contributed to the development of this knowledge. These professionals use Japanese terms—although some have identical English equivalents—some of which are explained below.

2.5.1 Kaizen

Kaizen means a changed attitude whereby people decide to take *quality* as their first priority in their work and personal life. An integral part of TQM is to build *quality* into *people* alongside the product or production process. It explains the importance of contribution from everybody to improvement of production process. Kaizen-consciousness can only be established when management is ready to change its culture.

2.5.2 Kamban System

This can be translated into "Just in Time System", or literally as "Sign Boards" or "Labels". The signboard is sent with the product to the next stage of the production process. When that next stage has started to put the product through its stage of the process, the signboard is sent back to the earlier stage. Only after the initial stage has received back its *kamban* can it produce further. The system tries to ensure that all necessary parts are received and delivered promptly only when they are needed, cutting down on waste, storage space and inventory.

2.5.3 Jidokha

The direct translation of this is *automation* and it means that the entire production system stops whenever a defect is identified in some part of the production process. It is usually achieved through electronic control over the production process. Only when the defect is corrected will the electronic system allow the process to resume. This system helps ensure that small defects do not lead to major losses in the final stages of the process.

2.5.4 Poke-Yoke

The literal translation of this term would be *defect* = *0*, and it can be considered as the equivalent of the 'zero defect' philosophy. Through this system detectors or inspectors are installed to identify mistakes, and whenever a mistake is identified the entire process is brought to a halt and the mistake corrected, only after the mistake is corrected is the system allowed to proceed.

2.5.5 Company Wide Quality Control

This is similar to the term *total quality management* introduced into Japanese industry by Professor Kaoru Ishikawa. He believed in the need to educate every worker in the company, from top to bottom, on the need for quality control.

2.6 TERMS FOR THE TQM SYSTEM

In some professions there is an internationally accepted nomenclature and terminology. All members of the medical profession use the International Classification of Diseases (ICD). All diagnosis must be written according to these regulations. Even though there are widely accepted norms in the terminology and nomenclature of management science, there is no internationally accepted system of classification. For example, a search of the literature shows that there are at least two different explanations for the difference between the terms, 'management' and 'administration'. The difficulties in quality management are even greater as it is a newly emerging field and that is not taught in the traditional management schools. This has led to a wide variation in terminology. Let us discuss some of the commonly accepted terms in quality management.

In day-to-day work, the following process is repeated again and again. Starting with a set of inputs, a defined process is worked, resulting in the production of an output. This is the same procedure whether a computer or a cup of tea is the end product. Chapter Four discusses this in greater detail. Some Quality Management terms in the context of the production process are discussed in what follows.

2.6.1 Quality Checking

This is the process of checking products for quality on the production line. Products are checked to ensure that they meet all expectations and requirements. The products that are checked in this way can be inputs, intermediate products or final products. Quality checks can also be performed on environmental factors that may influence the quality of the product. Checking can be done mechanically or with electronic devices, or manually with the help of such devices. Either every item or a few can be checked using an appropriate sampling technique.

2.6.2 Quality Inspectors

Quality inspectors are responsible for the effective implementation of quality checking. They are usually technicians with a clear understanding of the production process and the importance of quality. Their responsibilities include assuring that quality checking devices function properly, training other quality checkers and ensuring that sampling is done correctly.

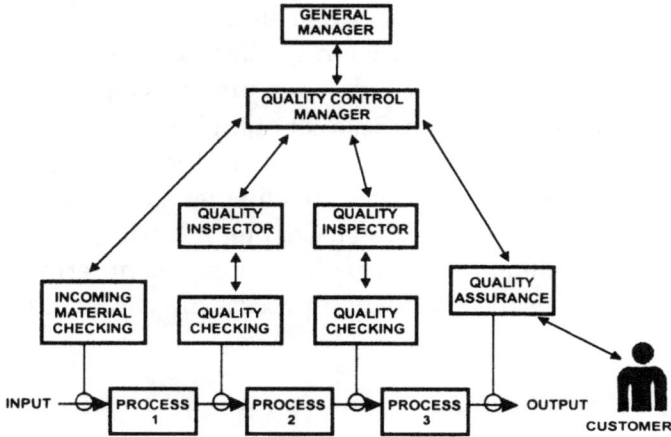

Fig. 2.5 A Quality Management System inside a Company

2.6.3 Quality Assurance

Quality inspectors are an important part of the quality management team, who ensure that customers receive defect-free goods. They are usually responsible for quality checking the final product and they usually do 100 per cent checking. The quality assurance team is also responsible for receiving and responding to customer problems and complaints and passing this information on to the appropriate people for corrective action. They also perform customer research whenever necessary.

2.6.4 Quality Control Manager

This is usually a middle management position, requiring a good understanding of the technology of the process. The manager receives feedback from quality inspectors, the quality assurance team and other employees and then coordinates with the necessary staff to guide, plan and implement a quality control process. The person in this position will communicate with the upper management and will have overall responsibility for quality management within the company.

2.6.5 Quality Circles

These are informal groups formed by employees doing similar work. Initially, they were formed in Japan. They usually consist of 8–10 members. The membership is voluntary. The groups work together on an equal basis: strengthening team spirit, helping in the setting and attainment of reasonable targets, improving morale and communication, promoting initiative and developing ability in problem-solving. Beyond these traditional informal groups, a wider group consisting of people from management and suppliers also can be formed. Whenever possible, representatives from customers should also be included.

With this brief introduction to quality management terms, let us move to a detailed discussion of quality management concepts.

Chapter Three

COMMITMENT TO CONTINUOUS IMPROVEMENT

3.1 PROBLEMS WITH COMMITMENT

Within the industry today, the most frequently used word is probably 'computer'. The next frequently used word is probably 'quality.' Despite this, 25–50 per cent of any standard quality management textbook will be devoted to problems regarding commitment to continuous improvement. More often than not, it is the upper management that gets the blame.

Although there is a widespread acceptance that quality is highly valued by customers and several textbooks have been written on how to achieve quality, there is still an unwillingness to change fundamental attitudes in order to achieve the goal. The following are some of the most common reasons for this failure.

3.1.1 Short-term Profit Motive

Even though customers respect a company on the basis of its quality, investors such as shareholders and banks only look at the profit margin or price of shares. Top management's immediate motive is to satisfy the shareholders. It is common practise to evaluate the credibility and efficiency of the top management by the price of shares, not by the quality of the products.

There are several ways to make a profit: cutting corners, closing down plants, encouraging 'voluntary' redundancies, cutting down on training, cutting down on the facilities available to employees, shipping everything in the stores without a care for quality and one step beyond this; shipping things that are not in the store, on paper, to show a greater profit. All of these methods can increase the price of shares and profit for a short period of time but slowly and steadily these measures will bring down the quality, leaving unsatisfied employees and consumers. This finally leads to the collapse and bankruptcy of the company.

Achieving quality should be a long-term goal for which short-term profit may need to be sacrificed. Without such determination, it is impossible to make products with quality.

3.1.2 Leaving Responsibility to the Lower Levels

Another reason for problems with commitment is that top managements try and evade responsibility for quality by saying that quality is an aspect of the production process and can only be achieved by people on the production line. Top-level management, therefore, fails to accept its responsibility while cutting resources for customer research and employee training and benefits, both of which are essential for motivation towards quality.

It must be understood that unless the upper management is ready to change its attitude and make the necessary investments to improve quality, nothing will be achieved.

3.1.3 Only Advertisements and Slogans

Upper management may choose a strategy of investing in advertising campaigns that stress quality and use slogans such as 'zero defect' in company worksheets while failing to invest in customer-research, employee-training and the other necessary steps to improve quality. This can be thought of as an attempt to cheat customers while unnecessarily annoying employees. The important truth that has to be understood is that if the customers feel cheated, their dissatisfaction will grow and this will lead to a bad reputation for the product within the market. Finally, there will be nothing left but the advertisement to recommend the product. A quality certificate cannot come from the producer or from an advertisement, it must come as appreciation from the customer.

3.1.4 Failure to Act Constantly

Another problem in implementing quality systems is that satisfaction with immediate results leads to abandonment of the system that produced the improvement. First, the necessary steps for quality improvement are taken: customer research, training, benefits for employees and so on, but when the resulting quality improvements lead to increasing sales and profits, the initial investment is withdrawn.

The main reasons for this type of behaviour are a failure to understand the importance of working continuously towards the goal of holding on to success and the short-term profit motive; an attempt to double the profit leads to greater losses in the long term. The important point to understand here is that once employees and customers lose their confidence in a company's long-term quality motive, it is difficult to win that confidence back.

3.1.5 Reluctance to Change Culturally

One of the most widely heard phrases about quality management is that it is 'a new culture'. If that is true, what is the difference between this new culture and the old one? A traditional management structure is an authoritarian organization run on a profit motive, whereas a quality management structure is an information organization run on a customer-satisfaction motive. A good quality manager should be a good communicator with access to a lot of information and patience to identify and satisfy customer needs.

A manager brought up in the old tradition will find it difficult to change towards this new direction while also dreading being left behind in the new revolution. As a result, a manager might try to block the quality revolution by refusing to change or refusing to implement changes on the site. However, it should be clearly understood that one person cannot stop a revolution and even if one company is slow to change another company will respond to the changes that are taking place in the market.

3.2 COST OF QUALITY

One of the most important reasons for delays in implementing a quality management system inside the company is the cost associated with it. When there is decreasing profit due to poor quality, trying to implement a quality management system that further reduces profit may cause the investors to panic.

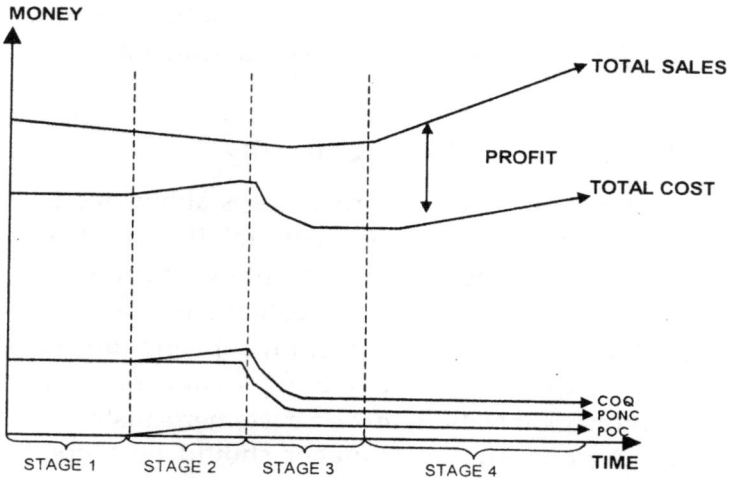

Fig. 3.1 Different Costs Incurred During Different Stages
of TQM Implementation

Are investors' fears reasonable, what are the possible
solutions for them? Chapter Two discussed some of the
costs related to quality. Figure 3.1 shows how these and
other figures can vary during the different stages of the
TQM implementation process.

The TQM implementation process can be divided
into four stages that are discussed in greater detail in
what follows.

Stage 1   This is the stage in which an organization
has no specific quality management
programme. The diagram shows total sales
and total expenditure, with the difference
in profit. Profit is shown as decreasing
because quality awareness usually arises only
when a company starts to lose its gains. Cost

of quality is shown as equal to the price of non-conformance as we assume that there is no specific quality management program inside (Price of Conformance = 0). The following equations will help make the figure easier to understand.

Profit = Total Sales – Total Expenditure

Cost of Quality = Price of Non-Conformance + Price of Conformance

Here PONC is shown as 25–30 per cent of the total sales as this is an accepted figure by quality management consultants, including Philip B. Crosby.

Stage 2   A company usually starts to implement a quality management program once it has started to lose profit. It is assumed that the company understands that it has a quality problem and begins to steadily implement a TQM program without pulling back. As the program is being implemented, there is a new cost, the price of conformance (POC). It increases the cost of quality and total expenditure. It is also too early to expect a drop in the price of non-conformance. If it is assumed that management understands the issues and does not make any early cut backs in quality expenditure, this stage can last from 6 months to 3 years, depending on the size of the organization and the types of problems that it has.

Stage 3   At this stage the company starts to see the early benefits of the programme; the price of non-conformance begins to fall, as does the cost of quality. Profits increase as a result of the fall in PONC. Sales are still at the same level as it is too early to see any increase in demand. This period may last for 1 or 2 years or more.

Stage 4   One of the long-term results of a constant quality management program is that the product gets a reputation for quality within the market. This leads to a greater number of orders and although expenditure increases in order to cope with the greater production, sales also increase, leading to greater profit.

The diagram makes several assumptions that cannot be made in a real company where the lines may move up and down unexpectedly depending on the market situation and changing commitment to the TQM process. However, the figure does provide an understanding of how profit, PONC and other money-related figures will change in different stages of TQM implementation.

While the TQM program is being implemented, there is a reduction in profit, at least for a temporary period. In this situation it helps to think of profit as a reward for the implementation of the program. The final result of quality management is not just profit; customer satisfaction, market share, improved employee morale and greater efficiency in operation are also gained. There will also be a reward in terms of better teamwork, effective communication, a happier working environment and improved working relations.

3.3 BREAKING THE BARRIERS

How can an organization break the barriers that stand in the way of a commitment towards continuous improvement?

- When trying to explain quality problems, using figures such as PONC or COQ can give an idea of the waste of money in different sections as a result of poor quality. Figures such as scrap value and percentage defects will not give upper management and investors a real idea of the magnitude of the problem or the true cost of defective items. Figures such as PONC will help the management understand how much money it can save by investing a small amount of time and money in quality management programs.

- Another method to gain upper management commitment to quality improvement is exposure to breaking news and case studies of the bankruptcy of well-established companies. Highlighting to investors and upper management the mistakes made by such companies will help change their attitude to TQM.

- Even after everyone has decided to implement TQM and started work towards it, there could be resistance and obstacles from some in middle or upper management who find it difficult to change. In such cases, it is important to find the causes of this type of behaviour. It is usually a case of unnecessary fear about the system or a lack of confidence in the system. Education can be used to remove fear, but once everything has been tried and there is no change, then some hard decisions have to be made that may include dismissal. Although such decisions are difficult, they may be the only ones available to protect customers, products and the company itself.

When implementing changes it is important to remember that while anybody can make a mistake, it is important to have the courage to take responsibility for the mistake and make the necessary changes to ensure that it will not happen again.

3.4 WE NEED TO CHANGE TODAY

Everyone must accept and understand that a new form of industrial revolution is before us, in the form of a quality revolution. The opening of new markets, greater competition for each product and the revolution in information management made possible by computers have all made this revolution both necessary and possible. Companies have to take notice and make changes, as a failure to do so will mean being washed away in the revolution.

Of course, what Deming's said remains true: "A big ship travelling at full speed requires distance and time to turn around." However, this should not be taken as an excuse for laziness or unnecessary delays in implementing changes. A ship that thinks it is a big monopoly and can therefore face any revolution without danger will be the next "Titanic". Even if this thought does not lead to change, a few more words from Deming might prove helpful: "You do not have to do this; survival is not compulsory." The Titanic experience did not put an end to sea travel and many smaller ships travelled in the same sea without danger by respecting Nature and its revolution.

3.5 COMMITMENT PROBLEMS IN THE SERVICE SECTOR

Commitment problems are more important in the service sector for several reasons. Usually the root causes of the problems are not easy to identify and will only become apparent when they have become severe and difficult to solve. Once the most common problems have been solved, finding the next important problem is not readily achieved.

While industry can suffer because of short-term profit motives, the service sector faces problems in using and implementing money-orientated measures. Although there are several other measurement indices, they are not always reliable. For example, while most governments give positive indications about a country's economic situation, the true picture will only emerge once there is a depression. The difficulty of implementing money-oriented indices leads to problems in implementing quality management measures inside the service sector.

Another problem in the service sector is in defining standard criteria. This allows the sector to produce advertisements claiming a quality service without having any basis in fact. A failure to act constantly and change culture alongside the problems outlined above are the difficulties encountered in trying to achieve a commitment to continuous improvement in the service sector.

Chapter Four

PRODUCTION:
UNDERSTANDING EVENTS

4.1 INTRODUCTION TO PRODUCTION PROCESS[8]

Most normal day-to-day work follows a standard pattern: a set of actions is performed upon a set of inputs to produce an output. Even when making a cup of coffee, this pattern is followed. We take coffee powder, water, milk and sugar and then boil the water, mix the coffee powder with the boiling water and then filter the mixture. After this, we mix milk and sugar to produce the final output—a cup of coffee. This process is called IPO (Input – Process – Output).

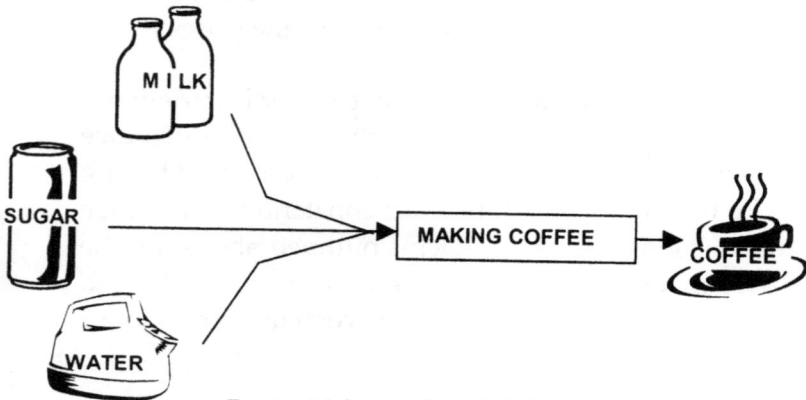

Fig. 4.1 Making a Cup of Coffee

Making a cup of coffee is a simple process that involves only one person where the input supplier and the output consumer are easy to identify. However, with a more advanced production process, such as making a computer or educating a student, the process will be more complicated and should be broken into smaller sub-processes that make the final product. The sub-processes may be completed by different companies or by different departments within the same company. In the industrial world the sub-processes will converge, starting with many different products and ending in one final completed product.

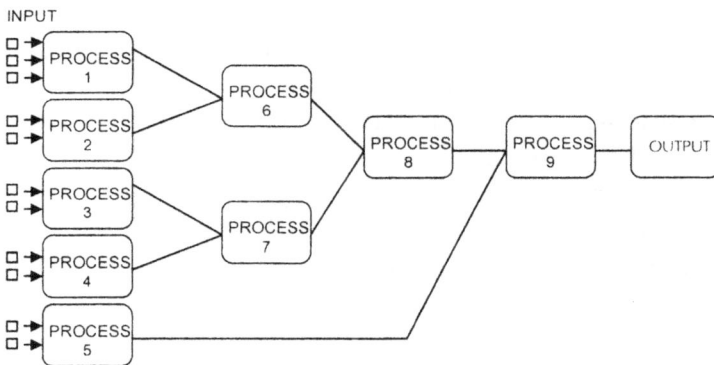

INPUT

Fig. 4.2 Production Process

4.2 CYCLES IN THE PRODUCTION AREA

General administration is usually taught as different functions—such as planning, organizing, implementing and controlling—although in real administration things are not so neatly divided into different areas. Planning is not usually just done once; during the implementation of the plan, the situation is evaluated and changes are

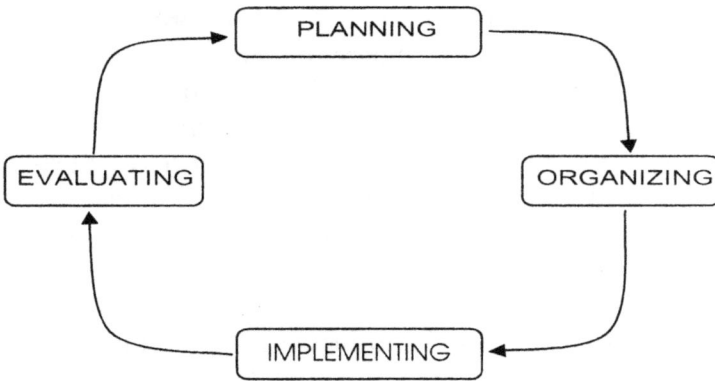

Fig. 4.3 Management Cycle

made to the original plan and organization. The changes depend on the market situation and customer expectations. It is more efficient to change the control function through evaluation and try to arrange all the different functions in a cycle.

Figure 4.3 gives an idea of the real relationship between different management functions inside a company or organization.

What about quality management? Are there any similar cycles in this new philosophy? In his book, Deming gives a cycle called the Deming Cycle (or the Shewhart Cycle as Deming prefers to call it) that also consists of four main stages.

Although 'Do' and 'Act' may look similar, Deming differentiates between them; he suggests that the 'do' stage is used to implement small-scale planned changes. In this stage, small tests should be conducted and the data collected. The data should be checked and resources organized for successful implementation.

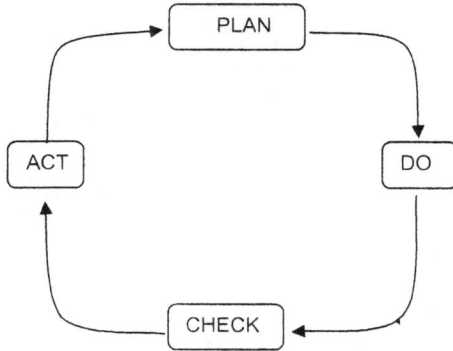

Fig. 4.4 Deming Cycle

What Deming has tried to do is replace the 'organization' function with a more practical and experimental 'do' function.

Chapter One listed seven different functions in quality management. Is there a similar cycle here? Although there is a relationship, there are no strict rules that define this relationship. Quality management requires jumping from one action to another and sometimes concentrating on particular actions depending on the situation within the company. The following diagram illustrates some possible relationships between the different functions of quality management with some equivalent general management functions.

4.3 THE PRODUCTION PROCESS AND THE HUMAN BODY

Philip B. Crosby starts his book *Quality Without Tears* with the following: "When a physician sees a patient with red spots, a fever, and a brother who has measles, it is not necessary to be Louis Pasture to make a

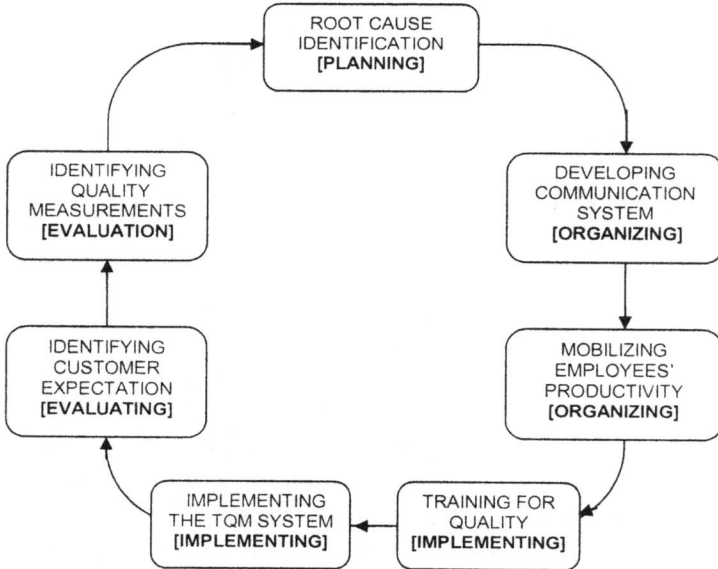

Fig. 4.5 Quality Management Cycle

diagnosis." In many instances, within his writing, Crosby compares the functioning of the human body with similar situations inside organizations to explain problems and provide solutions. As a member of the medical profession, the author would like to elaborate the analogy and try and explain some quality management functions.

A study of a textbook on human physiology will show how various systems, such as the hormonal and nervous systems coordinate the functions of every single cell in the body to work in cooperation for the effective survival of the body. While every single cell receives information from other parts of the body for its function, it also gives support to other parts of the body whenever there is a need. There are millions of cells in the human body and they are organized into seven or more different systems and as eight or more different body parts. A comparable organization, even a multinational company, will not have millions of employees; the maximum in such instances would be about 100,000 employees. How do so many cells function together without any hassle to produce a wonderful organization that cannot be reproduced in society? Some knowledge about the human body will help organize companies more efficiently.

4.3.1 Communication Systems of Our Body

Ask a high school student of Biology, 'what is the communication system of the body?' and he might reply 'the nervous system'. Of course, the brain, spinal cord, nerves and sensory organs form the important part of the communication system of the body. More importantly however, the cells inside the body use chemical substances to communicate with each other. It may be hormones released by special cells inside the body and transmitted by blood or toxins, chemicals released by dying cells. All of these communication systems inside the body can be categorized into three groups: local, regional and central according to their functions. Let us discuss this classification in a little more detail.

When a single germ enters the body through the skin on a fingertip, the brain and central immune system do not have to come into action to remove that germ. White blood cells that circulate in the local area identify the germ through differences on its cell membrane and remove it. Even if there are too many germs and the local white cells are unable to remove them, the central immune system is still not necessary. Chemical substances released from the interaction between germs and white blood cells dilate local blood vessels. As a result, there is a greater flow of blood and more while cells come into the area until the problem is effectively dealt with. It is only if the problem still remains that the central immune system is brought into play.

This example gives several lessons that can be used to improve the organization of companies. The first message is the importance of decentralization of communication systems and decision-making authority within the company. In order to identify and solve non-conformance problems effectively, authorized personnel should be present to identify and solve problems on site. If the solution to every problem has to await the decision of a central committee, a huge pile of problems will result.

The second lesson is that like the body using toxins released from dying cells to communicate problems, a company can use scrap materials that are produced by mistake as a means of communication. This form of communication can function in addition to the money-oriented evaluation system to help identify problems more effectively.

4.3.2 The Immune System of the Body

How does the immune system identify incoming germs and remove them? If a company could install a similar surveillance system it could be used to identify non-conforming materials.

In the body the white blood cells check cells that they come across using a certain chemical code. The cells that do not have a matching code or have a different code are removed instantly. The idea of a chemical code can be used to develop a checklist that will identify non-conforming materials in production. Another important lesson is that the white cells do not check every single cell. They check cells on a random basis but the sampling ratio increases when they come across non-conforming cells. If there is a need the sampling ratio can go up to 100 per cent for effective functioning. This model of a defect sensitive surveillance system can be introduced to make quality checking more efficient.

4.3.3 The Genetic Code of the Body

Another important example that can be drawn from the body is the genetic code. All the information necessary to build the body is recorded in the genetic code. It is through this code that information is passed from generation to generation. Similar information systems have been built for companies in the form of intranets. Process manuals necessary to build products can be developed and stored on computers so that they can be accessed from any corner of the company whenever necessary.

An important feature of genetic codes is mutation or accidental changes in the genetic code that lead to changes in the body. Even though this example cannot be directly translated into the context of the company, it does show the importance of making changes in the process manuals in order to improve.

4.4 THE PRODUCTION PROCESS IN THE SERVICE SECTOR

The service sector is similar to the industrial in that a whole service is produced as a result of several sub-processes although the sub-processes are usually arranged in a manner different to that found in the industry. Instead of a converging pattern where several different products are used to make a single product, there is one product processed through different processes at different times, or a single product processed sub-processes at the same time and released as a single product.

(A)

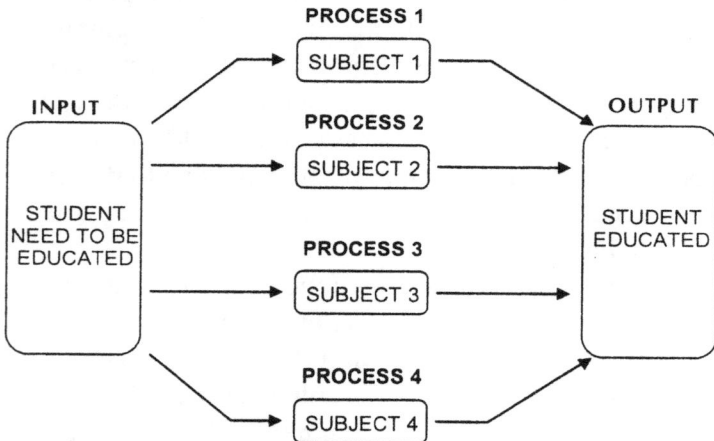

(B)

Fig. 4.6. The Production Process in the Service Sector

The discussion so far should help towards a better understanding of the production process. The real time example will be much more complicated as thousands of different services and products may be involved in a single process. To produce a good quality product, each of the different tasks has to be performed properly. This is the fundamental fact that has to be understood before a quality management system is implemented in a company.

Chapter Five

UNDERSTANDING CUSTOMER EXPECTATIONS

5.1 CUSTOMER EXPECTATIONS

One of the most important quality management concepts is 'customer satisfaction'. In today's market a customer making a purchase decision is faced with a great deal of choice. This makes him/her focus on quality. What does quality mean for the customer? This varies from customer to customer. Some customers look for accountability, others for price. As we have seen in Chapter Two, these expectations can be grouped into the four as:

- Accountability
- Affordability (Price)
- Availability
- Appearance

When we buy a product we want it to perform certain functions. Only when we are satisfied with the functions of the product for an expected time period do we accept the product is accountable. After we are satisfied with accountability, sometimes even before that, we check whether the product is affordable. The third thing customers look for is whether the product will be available for use as soon as it is bought. Finally, some customers place more emphasis on the appearance of the product. Which out of the four is the most important varies from customer to customer and from situation to situation; therefore, it is the customer who defines quality. Let us explore in detail the four elements of quality.

5.1.1 Accountability

When a product or service is able to perform its expected functions without any problems, it is considered accountable. How does a customer come to think that a product is accountable? Usually by advice from friends or people he or she considers reliable. Accountability is therefore not easy for a company to achieve. Only the customers themselves can give a certificate of accountability. Are there any other ways to achieve it?

There are a number of methods that can be used to achieve a reputation for quality when introducing a new product in the market: issuing free products on a random basis, delivering trial products for a trial period, showing test performances in public places and finally by giving a warranty. The important thing about the reputation for accountability is that once it is lost, it is almost impossible to regain. Companies must also remember that more and more quality products are entering the market every day and unless the accountability of a product or service is regularly updated, the market can be lost at any time.

5.1.2 Affordability (Price)

An important aspect of any product is its price. The traditional belief that low price means low quality and high price means high quality no longer applies. An efficient defect-prevention mechanism inside the company makes it possible to deliver good quality goods at a lower price than would be expected. Japanese goods are reliable but also have a low price. When introducing a new product, low price is a useful technique to capture the market. The ability to deliver good quality goods at a low price is the prime secret to success.

5.1.3 Availability

When consumers buy a product they expect it to be immediately available for their use. It is possible to send an order for a product from anywhere in the world within a fraction of a second. It is also becoming possible to send products anywhere in the world within a week. The traditional view that an efficient marketing management system is important for the success of any business still holds true. A company that wants to capture and maintain customers must have an efficient marketing system.

5.1.4 Appearance

Perhaps more importantly than the elements discussed earlier, the appearance of a product plays an important role in satisfying customer expectations. Usually this is a feature of customer likes and dislikes. It could be related to the product's colour or shape. To achieve customer satisfaction in this regard, the company must be ready to release every technology that it produces with different appearances and colours. Such attempts will help satisfy a wide variety of expectations. In some instances the ability to deliver products at short notice to a consumer who wants it in an unusual colour or shape may help improve customer relations.

In discussing customers, it is also important to mention customers who show violent behaviour towards the employees. It is usually in the service sector that one comes across such customers. Whenever such problems are encountered, the most senior person on site should handle such abusive customers and try calming them down to find out what happened.

If the problem was caused by an employee who had acted irresponsibly or delayed the customer for an unreasonable period of time, then appropriate action should be taken. This could include employing more staff to prevent such delays or training employees in customer relations. If the senior member of staff is not able to calm the customer down or if it is found that the customer had purposefully made the mistake, then the incident should be reported to the appropriate law enforcing authority to take appropriate action. Trying to be lenient with such customers not only disappoints the employees but also other customers who want to use the services in a peaceful environment.

5.2 NEW IDEAS ABOUT CUSTOMERS[8]

Traditionally, the word *customer* means a person outside the company who buys the company's products or services. In quality management, however, the word customer has other meanings. Chapter Four introduced the idea that in the real world products come together as a result of the hundreds of small different actions inside the company. In quality management these actions are seen as separate processes with the person at the beginning of the process treated as a supplier and the person at the end, the customer. According to this model, everyone inside the company will be a supplier and a customer at the same time.

While the customers inside the company are called internal customers, our traditional customer outside the company is called the external customer. This model helps establish conformance requirements for each sub-product in order to achieve a better quality final output. The following figure may explain this concept more clearly.

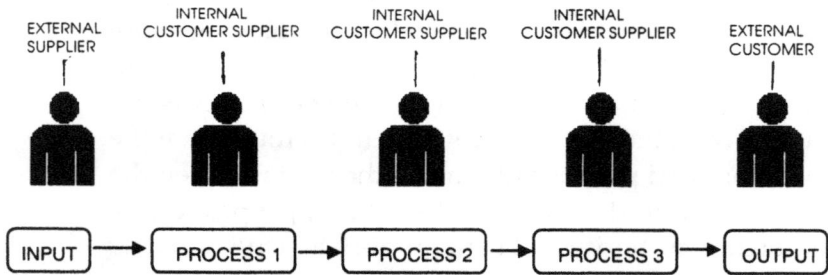

| INTERNAL | INTERNAL | INTERNAL |
| EXTERNAL SUPPLIER | CUSTOMER SUPPLIER | CUSTOMER SUPPLIER | CUSTOMER SUPPLIER | EXTERNAL CUSTOMER |

INPUT → PROCESS 1 → PROCESS 2 → PROCESS 3 → OUTPUT

Fig. 5.1 Relationship of the Internal Customer
and the Internal Supplier

This model sees every employee inside the company as a supplier and customer at the same time. Even though it is philosophically correct if you try to implement practically, it can create a lot of confusion. Usually each department or each quality management unit is considered a customer by the previous unit and as a supplier for the next unit.

A further type of consumer is the 'indirect customer'. Take a simple day-to-day example—everyone in a house being served food on time by the mother. This does not mean that she serves everybody all the time; she might ask someone, for example one of the children, to make coffee for guests or dad. The children will not then take the coffee to the mother who will give it to the person; they will give it to the person themselves. Here the mother is an indirect customer. The following figure may explain this idea more clearly.

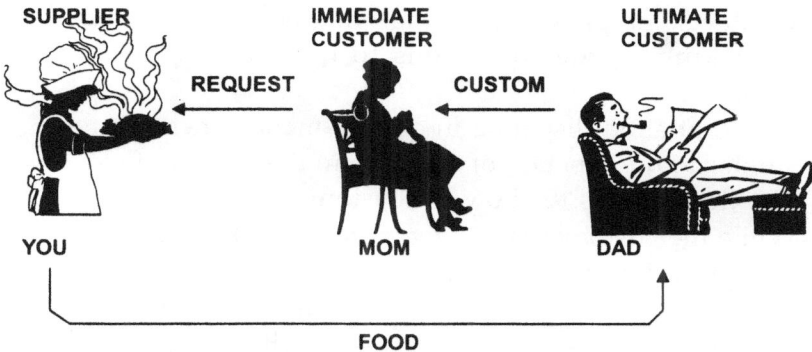

Fig. 5.2 Immediate and Ultimate Customers Inside the Home

In the world outside, a similar relationship can be identified between people, government or government servants.

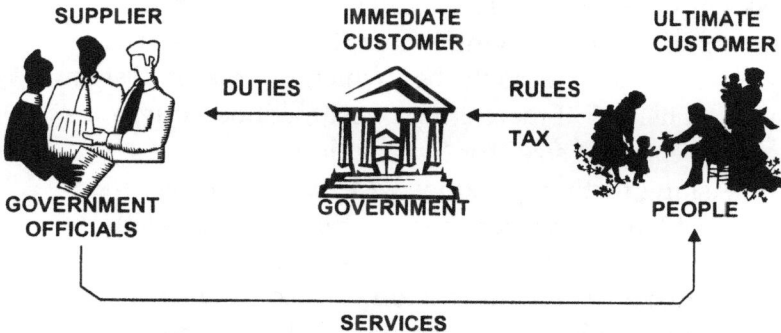

Fig. 5.3 Immediate and Ultimate Customers in Society

5.3 COMMUNICATION WITH CUSTOMERS

In the medical world, many of the patient's problems are identified by listening to the patient. Further examinations and investigations are performed to either confirm the diagnosis or solve the small percentage of remaining unsolved problems. However, listening in medicine does not just mean passively listening to whatever the patient is saying; the doctor follows up by asking further questions to get more detailed information.

What about listening in quality management? It is similar to the function of listening in the medical field. The first thing is to allow the customer to speak freely. While the customer is talking, notes must be taken. Of course if the customer is communicating through a letter or e-mail, there is no need to take notes. This process will give an idea of the nature of the customer's complaint.

The next step is to ask further questions. The customer's complaint or request may not contain all of the necessary information to find out the cause of the problem or satisfy the customer's request. Only by asking further questions we can solve this problem. For example, when receiving a complaint about software, a further question could be: 'which operating system are you using?' If there is a request for shoes, questions could be, 'what size?' or 'what colour?'

Asking further questions will give a clear picture of the problem. However, it may still not be possible to act. Everyone is subject to error, something could have been missed from the customer's complaint or the complaint could be misinterpreted. It is important to restate to the customer everything that has been recorded and the solutions that are planned. When ending a conversation with the customer, it is important to have a closing question. Some examples of closing questions could be: 'Do you have any other problem?' or 'Is there anything else you need to buy?' These questions can lead to another listen, question and restate cycle.

Communicating with customers about the plan that will be used to solve their problem will lead to greater cooperation from the customers. This idea has greater acceptance in the medical and educational fields where the cooperation of patients and students in solving problems and implementing solutions is seen as very important.

5.4 IDENTIFYING CUSTOMER EXPECTATIONS

Three different types of customers have been identified: internal, external and intermediate. When trying to identify customer expectations, even though all three types of customers are important, it is not so difficult with internal or immediate customers as they are mostly within arms reach or have a clear and established relationship with the company. But identifying the expectations of the external customer is more difficult and more challenging for a quality control manager. Here we can see ways to identify external customer expectations. Identifying internal customer expectation will be explained in detail in the next chapter.

What is the best way to collect data on external customers' dissatisfaction? A number of different methods are used that can be categorized into three basic groups.

1. Regular customer communication channels
2. Occasional customer research
3. Other customer-related information

It is usually the responsibility of the quality assurance section, within the quality management department, to collect information about external customer expectations and pass it on to the appropriate authority.

When gathering information from customers, it is important that customers should not simply be viewed as the target of a sales pitch, to be forgotten once the sale has been made; long-term customer satisfaction should be the priority. Clearly this satisfaction can only come with a quality product and a proper after-sales-service. Customers' complaints should be viewed as an opportunity for improvement, and should never be ignored. Losing customer complaints means losing valuable information and creating obstacles for improvement. Customers should be treated with respect and products should be sold on quality, not price. The first objective should be to achieve quality, the second to reduce costs. When quality is present, profits, market share and low production costs also be present. With this in mind, let us will now explore the different methods to collect customer information.

5.4.1 Regular Customer Communication Channels

The best method of identifying customer expectations is to allow every single customer to communicate his/her complaint directly, whenever he/she have one. Such regular communication can be achieved by giving an address or e-mail address with every product. In North

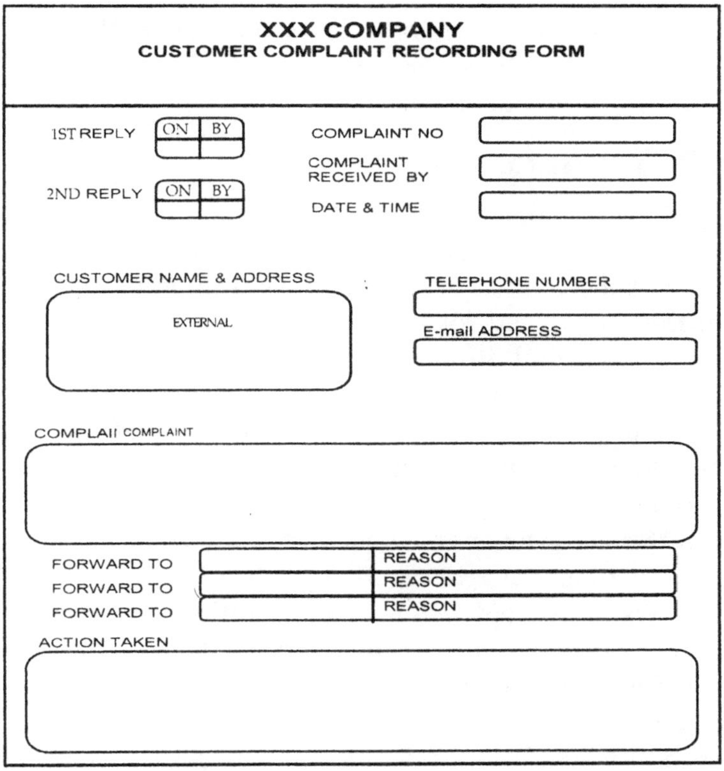

Fig. 5.4 Customer Complaint Recording Form

America, 1-800 series telephone numbers are used for this purpose alone. In stores and shops, such information can be printed on the back of receipts. These methods will identify dissatisfaction and complaints from customers on a regular basis.

When using such a communication channel, it is important to keep all documents regarding complaints and send back two replies to the person who made the complaint. The first should be sent once the complaint has been received to the appropriate department and the second once the corrective action has been taken. The form below gives some idea of how customer comments can be documented.

5.4.2 Occasional Customer Research

Alongside the regular communication channels, it is also a good idea to carry out some occasional customer research. The research is occasional as it is only done when there is a need for more information regarding customers without studying every single customer. Instead, a few customers are chosen using appropriate sampling techniques and a detailed study is conducted of their likes and dislikes and personal hobbies. This will be discussed in greater detail in Chapters Twelve and Thirteen. For the moment let us briefly see how we can conduct customer research.

The first thing to do is prepare a questionnaire that will help understand a wide range of customer expectations. Chapter Six will give some idea of what type of questions to ask. Before launching the research, it is useful to perform a pilot study that will evaluate the efficiency of the questionnaire. After the pilot study there may be a need to perform some minor modifications on the questionnaire before finalizing it. Once this has been done, there are two choices.

The first choice is to post or e-mail the questionnaire on a wide basis and base the research on the answered questionnaires. Poor response may be a problem and one way to overcome it is to offer a small sum of money (with such methods), but again there is the risk of biased information.

The second method available is to select customers by using an appropriate sampling technique. The sample should give a good estimate of the actual population of customers. Interviewers who will fill in such questionnaires on an appropriate basis must also be appointed. The interviewers will approach the selected customers and after getting their consent will fill in the questionnaire. If a customer cannot be reached or does not want to participate in the survey, another customer has to be selected using the same sampling technique.

After collecting this information, it has to be summarized and used to prepare a report about the customers. Although some companies like to keep such information confidential as they consider it important business information, it must be made available to planners inside the company when they need it. On top of such occasional research the occasional experimental release of defective goods or sending checkers pretending to be customers can also help ensure that employees are acting on non-conformance or intimidating situations appropriately.

5.4.3 Customer Related Information from Other Sources

Alongside the above information collected by the quality assurance department, information can also be gathered from many marketing research institutions outside the company. Such institutions conduct studies on a regular basis about public taste over different products. Even though such information may not give any specific information about the product, when combined with information collected by the company, it can be a useful guide. Information from marketing research companies can give valuable information about future investment. Also, when a new business is started, these companies may provide the only source of information that will help understand customer expectations in that area.

5.5 CUSTOMERS IN THE SERVICE SECTOR

Although there are some basic similarities between customers in the service and industrial sector, there are also a few differences. When receiving complaints from customers in the service sector, there may be no similarity between any of the complaints. The root cause of the problem may be the same but different people will experience it in a different way and will therefore have different complaints. In such situations, recording customers' complaints in their own words will be important in trying to find the root cause of the problems.

One advantage in the service sector is that most of the time customers have direct contact with their service providers. Expect a few instances where services are provided through brokers, in every other instance customers contact service companies directly to acquire their services. This makes it easy for service companies to identify customer complaints or conduct customer research.

Chapter Six

FINDING A MEASUREMENT SYSTEM

6.1 MEASUREMENT CHALLENGES

Having discussed ways to discover customer dissatisfaction, the next challenge is to translate that dissatisfaction in a technical language that will help to plan corrective action. This task is associated with finding measurements that will help understand customer dissatisfaction and productivity. It has two parts; the first is to list the conformance and non-conformance areas along the production line, the second is to change non-conformance to money values such as PONC so that upper administration and investors can understand the amount of money that is being lost through non-conformance.

There are a number of challenges to be faced when trying to achieve this task. In the history of medicine the first person who tried to measure the pulse and respiratory rate of humans was criticized for trying to damage the values of medicine. But scientists who came in later almost decided that anything could be measured. This attitude is expressed in Lord Kelvin's dictum: "Whatever exists, exists in some quantity and can therefore be measured."

Today, not only in medicine but also in several other fields there are measurement indices that help solve problems. Any news or information that is not accompanied by a measurement index can only be considered as an opinion. When information is attached to a figure or measurement index, it becomes useful data or a fact.

However, in the social sciences, such as politics or administration, there are still difficulties in finding good measurement scales. Money represents a good measurement scale but in some instances it might not be useful and could actually mislead. The Management Consultant Philip B. Crosby tried to replace the money orientated profit index with PONC to calculate the efficiency of management. It is a good index from the upper management point of view.

The price of conformance (POC) and the price of non-conformance (PONC) are good indices to calculate the cost of quality; they are briefly discussed in the introduction but greater detail can be found in Crosby's books *Quality is free* and *Quality Without Tears*. An accounting index, other than profit, that can be considered useful for quality analysis is 'costing and cost ascertainment'.

6.1.1 Costing and Cost Ascertainment[9]

The origins of this measurement index lie in the First World War, when governments gave industrial organizations producing materials for the war effort a certain assurance in the form of 'cost plus' prices that would ensure a reasonable profit. Industry was expected to find the cost of producing each product and government used the system of cost accounting to ensure that costs thus calculated were correct. Thus, the system of cost accounting was developed during the First World War in Britain.

The cost of a product can be divided into different cost elements; the cost element is the typical expenditure for one unit. All costs are calculated for one unit being processed. For a factory, the unit might be a car, for a school a student and for a hospital a patient. Costing helps administration in two ways: first it helps calculate the amount of profit that can be expected from each unit of production, secondly it helps quality management personnel identify wastage or costs of specific areas for better planning. For example, in the service sector, it is accepted that administrative costs should be kept at below 3–5 per cent; higher costs should be investigated and controlled.

The cost element and cost structure of a product are given below:

Cost element	$/Unit
Direct material	
Direct labour	
Direct expenses	
Prime cost	
Production or factory overheads	
Production cost	
Administrative cost	
Selling and distribution	
Total cost of sales	
Profit	
Sale price	

A detailed explanation of each of these is beyond the scope of this book; a standard accountancy book will furnish more details. The utility of this method will be seen if costing information is used for planning.

6.2 NON-MONEY-ORIENTATED TQM INDICES

These indices will not be the same for all departments or for all industries. It will be different from department to department and even from technology to technology. Usually the conformance and non-conformance lists— this will be discussed shortly—that come between departments will be used as quality measurement indices. In addition there will be measurement indices for management personnel and services. These will be discussed in greater detail in section 'Measurement Indices for the Service Sector'. The following give an idea of good measurement indices for a supervisor.

1. Employee turnover
2. Number of sick leaves
3. Reported conflicts between employees.

Officers from different sectors, including medical, civil service, health, immigration and so on are often happy to see queues in front of their offices. They feel that this shows that lots of people want to see them; they are VIPs and so on. It must be remembered that everything that is lost can be regained except time. Wasting time, either another's or one's own, should be considered the biggest blunder that a manager can make. Chapter Two defined management as 'making decisions'. Of course making good decisions is good management and making bad decisions may be one step below, but not making decisions at all in the allotted time means no management at all.

Let us now discuss satisfying the internal customer by preparing conformance and non-conformance lists. One of the most common reasons given for low quality is low quality input. Even though management might not readily accept this, without providing good inputs you cannot expect good quality outputs; this might be a good broom for the cleaner or hardware for the computer. This problem causes a lot of conflict between departments inside an organization. How is this problem to be solved and who is to decide the quality of inputs and outputs: professional bodies, marketing departments or management?

As discussed in the previous chapter, it is the customers who would define quality. If this philosophy is accepted inside the company then problems can be resolved easily. An efficient way of achieving acceptance on quality requirements is to bring customers and suppliers to the table along with other people who can influence decision-making: the quality management team, professional bodies and so on. In such situations the customers can explain what they want and the supplier can explain any problems in attaining that. The management and technical people will try and provide the suppliers with what they need to achieve the requirement.

Once agreement is reached, there is no need for further conflict. Everyone's responsibility is to confirm that requirements are met. When a system is successfully developed to define requirements inside the company the following will start to happen: lowering of hassle level, suddenly voices drop, discussion is more orderly and the problems of quality are resolved without emotion. The other area that will show obvious improvement is the administration: actions become smoother, paperwork less cumbersome and long-standing confusion over procedures and processes is resolved.

After the requirements have been agreed on, the next task is to employ, train and manage quality checkers; the quality management department will perform this task. Quality checkers will ensure that customers receive only the products that meet their requirements and will ensure that information about non-conformance is recorded and passed back to the supplier for necessary corrective action to be taken. Who will manage the activities of quality checkers for better functioning of the system? Certainly the quality management department will have a role but who is going to be the next group, the customers or the suppliers?

If suppliers have an involvement they can get information about non-conformance immediately and can take the necessary corrective action. But there are chances that non-conforming products will escape and this will lead to complaints from customers about the performance of quality checkers. It is best therefore if customers manage the quality checkers with arrangements to pass back information about non-conformance to the supplier through a computerized information management system. Using these ideas about quality checking, let us now discuss how to build a quality management skeleton inside the company.

6.3 BUILDING A TQM SKELETON

Using this knowledge of quality management and quality checking it is possible to develop a quality management skeleton inside the company. The type of skeleton will depend on how big the company is and what type of problems it faces. The questionnaire in Appendix C will help companies decide if they need a quality management system. Is there a minimum size a company must reach before quality management ideas can be implemented? Some quality management ideas can be useful even in personal life.

Institutions working with two or three people can improve their performance by implementing quality management principles inside the company. It is not necessary to hire a quality management consultant or buy a big computerized data management system. All that is necessary is to record all information about non-conformance that is received. A small data management system, such as MS Access, can be used to computerize and analyze such data. There will be a further discussion on data base management systems in Chapter Fourteen. Once this has been done all employees should get together and discuss corrective action.

How can a moderate to large company build a quality management system. The chapter on 'production process' shows that a complicated product comes as a result of many small different actions. Quality management is not an exception to that. In order to implement quality management functions inside a big company, the first thing to do is to divide the company into different identifiable sections so that information about quality can be stored, analyzed and improvement processes implemented efficiently.

It is usually better to consider each department as a separate quality management unit but it does not have to be so strict. It is possible that one department can be divided into two quality management units or two departments can be joined to make one quality management unit. The division of departments should make it easy to collect and analyze data regarding quality.

What has to be accepted after different quality management units have been identified is that each unit is going to work as a customer for the previous section, giving conformance criteria, while working as a supplier for the next section on the production line and supplying products according to its expectations. It should be obvious that quality checking will be implemented between different units.

The chapter on 'Implementation' will discuss this in greater detail. Whether on-line or off-line inspection, whether zero defect or acceptable quality level, we can analyze there in more detail, but before moving further let us see if the probability of defective goods can be ascertained on the production line a particular situation. It is established that the final product is made as a result of assembling several smaller parts. Imagine a production line in which the final product is made as a result of assembling 100 different parts. Suppose a 1 per cent defect ratio is accepted for each part, what would be the probability of a defect in the final product? The probability ranges from 1 per cent to 100 per cent depending on how the defective parts are put together for the final product. The real figure may be something in between. The important fact that has to be understood is that trying to accept any defect in the production line will lead to a greater magnitude of problems in the next line and in addition will cause unnecessary money and time wastage.

6.4 MEASUREMENTS IN THE SERVICE SECTOR

With regard to measurements the service sector has some advantages and some disadvantages. The service sector, such as the health sector, has good measurement scales for its functions. It may be heart rate or temperature to analyze individual problems or infant mortality rate and life expectancy to understand the efficiency of the overall system. However, in other sectors, such as the civil service and government, there are many problems in identifying appropriate measurement scales. Only people working in these sectors and their customers can help each other to find appropriate measurement scales. The following list may help you to get an idea of measurement scales for different service sector personnel.

For telephone customer services:

- Time taken to answer each call.
- The number of attempts to solve each problem.

For a police department:

- Crime detection time.
- Number of crimes prevented.

For government services:

- Waiting time for service users.
- Number of problems solved.

With this idea about measurement, we can see how to analyze the information we have collected so far with the help of quality management tools.

Chapter Seven

RECORDING NON-CONFORMANCE AND IDENTIFYING ROOT CAUSES

7.1 RECORDING NON-CONFORMANCE

The previous chapter on 'measurement' showed that it is the duty of quality assurance people and quality checkers to check products against a requirements list and ensure that they are all achieved. While quality people pass conforming goods to the next stage of production, they will also need to do an important job with non-conforming products. They must record information about non-conforming material in an organized manner so that it can be analyzed and the necessary corrective action can be taken. How and where should this information be recorded?

7.1.1 Checksheets

Instruments or tools called *checksheets* are used for this purpose. Checksheets are designed for the purpose of recording either conformance or non-conformance. Checksheets used to record stock or the functions of a machine can be thought of as conformance checksheets.

Checksheets recording non-conformance can be used for two purposes: one for recording non-conformance in a product and the second for recording non-conformance regarding a process or machine. A checksheet used to record the non-conformance of a product usually has four parts:

1. General information and information about the department.
2. Information about the product and process.
3. Records about non-conformance.
4. List of non-conformance issues that need to be reported.

The first part, general information and information about the department, indicates the department using the checksheet and the quality checking section responsible for recording non-conformance as well as the name or ID of the quality checkers recording non-conformance.

The section on information about product and process records product ID, processes that are being performed, personnel involved, machine numbers used for the process and date and time of processes that are performed. This should make it clear that checksheets are not prepared at the quality checking point once the product has arrived but are produced when products are ready to travel through the assembly line. These checksheets travel with the product and every operation performed with all the necessary details are recorded on the production line.

The records about non-conformance will be filled by the quality checkers. They will record non-conformance in the appropriate spaces. The fourth part will contain the list of non-conformance issues that need to be checked. Figure 7.1 gives a sample checksheet. When the products are small and a single person processes many products each day then checksheets can

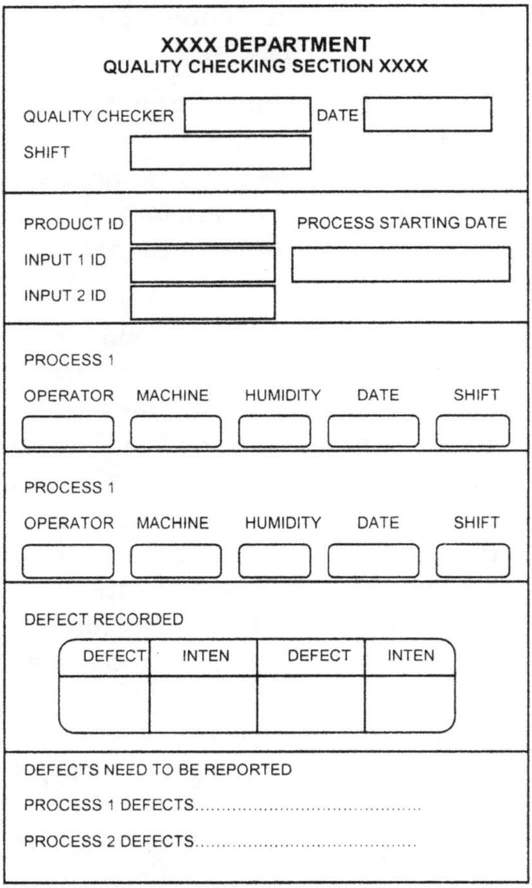

```
┌─────────────────────────────────────────────────────┐
│                  XXXX DEPARTMENT                      │
│            QUALITY CHECKING SECTION XXXX              │
│                                                       │
│   QUALITY CHECKER  [        ]    DATE  [        ]     │
│   SHIFT            [            ]                      │
├───────────────────────────────────────────────────────┤
│   PRODUCT ID  [          ]    PROCESS STARTING DATE   │
│   INPUT 1 ID  [          ]    [                 ]     │
│   INPUT 2 ID  [          ]                            │
├───────────────────────────────────────────────────────┤
│   PROCESS 1                                           │
│   OPERATOR  MACHINE   HUMIDITY    DATE     SHIFT      │
│   [      ]  [      ]  [      ]  [      ]  [      ]    │
├───────────────────────────────────────────────────────┤
│   PROCESS 1                                           │
│   OPERATOR  MACHINE   HUMIDITY    DATE     SHIFT      │
│   [      ]  [      ]  [      ]  [      ]  [      ]    │
├───────────────────────────────────────────────────────┤
│   DEFECT RECORDED                                     │
│   ┌────────┬────────┬────────┬────────┐              │
│   │ DEFECT │ INTEN  │ DEFECT │ INTEN  │              │
│   ├────────┼────────┼────────┼────────┤              │
│   │        │        │        │        │              │
│   └────────┴────────┴────────┴────────┘              │
├───────────────────────────────────────────────────────┤
│   DEFECTS NEED TO BE REPORTED                         │
│   PROCESS 1 DEFECTS.................................  │
│   PROCESS 2 DEFECTS.................................  │
└───────────────────────────────────────────────────────┘
```

Fig. 7.1 Checksheet for a Product

be prepared for a batch of products instead of single products.

Similar checksheets can be prepared to record the non-conformance of a machine or process. Here the structure will be modified according to convenience. A sample checksheet for a process is shown in Figure 7.2.

XXXX DEPARTMENT
QUALITY CHECKING SECTION XXXX

QUALITY CHECKER [ ]   DATE [ ]

SHIFT [ ]

PROCESS ID [ ]

NON-CONFORMANCE NEED TO BE REPORTED	OCCURANCE								
	DATE			DATE			DATE		
	SHIFT 1	SHIFT 2	SHIFT 3	SHIFT 1	SHIFT 2	SHIFT 3	SHIFT 1	SHIFT 2	SHIFT 3
NON-CONFORMANCE 1									
NON-CONFROMANCE 2									
NON-CONFORMANCE 3									
OTHER									

Fig. 7.2 Checksheet for a Process or Machine

Checksheets should be designed by those who have a good understanding of the process. A checksheet should record not only all non-conformance issues but also all other factors that can influence the quality of the product. For example, operator, machine, date and so on. Care must be taken to ensure that unnecessary information that does not influence quality is not recorded as this leads to time wastage at all levels and can lead to reduced compliance with data entry.

7.1.2 Control Charts[3]

Another important tool used to record conformance and non-conformance is the control chart. Control charts are mainly used to record a variable—a measurement that varies randomly within a limit. This variable can be either an environmental factor that can affect quality, for example temperature, or a measurement that can help determine the quality of the product, for example the power of a bulb.

The control chart was invented by Walter Shewhart whose work in the late 1920s initially focused on the reduction of variability in the performance of telephones at Bell laboratories. However, Deming realized the Shewhart's ideas were capable of much wider application and developed them further. What eventually came about is known as *performance indicator* (an indicator that helps determine quality) calculated over a time period. Plotting the performance measures on a chart may produce a pattern on the basis of which appropriate action can be taken.

The chart has a central line — calculated average over a time and an upper control limit and lower control limit. While the sample results vary randomly between the upper and lower limits, the process is deemed to be under control. This stable state is called *state of statistical control*, a state where variation, although still existent, is controllable and predictable. Non-random behaviour lines going outside this area require immediate corrective action to bring the process back to a stable state. Figure 7.3 shows an example of a control chart.

This chart can be used to take action at appropriate times so that the process variation is minimized and major problems are prevented in the future. The type of action we have to take depends on whether the cause of variation is controlled (common) or uncontrolled (special).

VARIABLE
TEMPERATURE

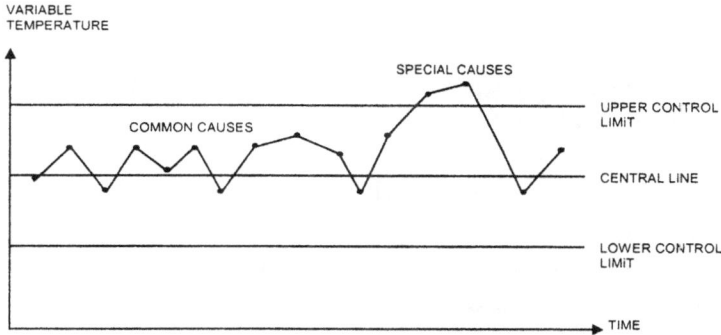

Fig. 7.3 SPC Control Chart

- **Controlled or Common Causes**
  There are many sources of variation within a process
  that are under statistical control. These include
  uncontrollable environmental conditions, the
  inflexibility of aged machines, variability of
  purchased material, component tolerance or other
  non-obvious causes of variation that may or may
  not be present at any one time but, when taken
  together, produce random results. To solve these
  common-cause problems action must be taken in
  accordance with a system. This is usually the
  responsibility of management who caused it. It
  requires change to the process itself.
- **Uncontrolled or Special Causes**
  Violation of the limits of a control chart, or the
  presence of a specific pattern within the control
  limits, indicates the existence of special causes of
  variation that are often easily recognizable. Such
  causes include changes of operator or shift, changes
  of raw materials, breakages, misreading of scales,
  occasional wrong setting of machines and so on.

These causes are not common to all the operations involved and so their discovery and removal require local action by personnel who are directly connected with operations.

The benefit of control charts is their ability to provide a common language that helps everyone in the organization avoid unnecessary tampering with the process and allows distinction between special and common causes, thus avoiding unnecessary blame and recrimination. Informed decisions can then be taken as to what sort of action is required and whose responsibility this action should be. Industrial experience suggests that only 15 per cent of process troubles are due to special causes and therefore correctable locally by people directly connected with the operation. The majority of problems—the remaining 85 per cent—are caused by common causes and correctable only by management action on the system.

7.2 STATISTICAL PROCESS CONTROL[3]

Before moving further, it is better to see what is meant by statistical process control. The control chart, discussed above, is the main tool of statistical process control (or SPC). The traditional method of quality control in manufacturing processes has been inspection of the final product. Usually 100 per cent inspection was performed but sampling inspection was also common. However, even a 100 per cent inspection did not guarantee 100 per cent reliability and, on some occasions, full inspection was carried out two or more times.

The traditional method was very expensive in time, money and manpower. As a result, the price of goods was rapidly increasing even though 100 per cent quality was not assured. To overcome this problem a valuable alternative was provided by the technique of statistical process control (SPC) that aims to prevent defective work being produced by focusing on the production process rather than on the final product.

The SPC process begins with the identification of several factors in the production line that can influence the quality of the final product. These factors could be either the quality of intermediate products or environmental factors that can have a bearing on the quality of products. Another important difference between SPC and traditional methods is that these factors are checked using appropriate electronic equipment. This equipment is either fully automatic or works with a minimum of manual assistance. The records from these checking stations are analyzed with the use of control charts, Pareto charts or any other quality tool to find the root cause of the problem.

Quality checking in SPC involves the selection of items using sampling techniques, but there is nothing strict about this. Whenever quality checking can be done with fully automatic electronic devises that are not too expensive, even 100 per cent checking can be performed. Although the technicalities of SPC have been known for some time and originated in America (Shewhart, 1931) it was Japanese industry that first proved the usefulness of SPC in practice.

7.3 ORGANIZATION OF DATA

The collection of quality data produced a bundle of sheets: checksheets, control charts and so on that contained important information about defective goods which could be used to improve processes. Before the information could be used it had to be organized so that relevant data could be accessed whenever needed. The sheets were sent to a clerical department where they were entered into a register so that a statistician could then analyze the data and produce necessary diagrams giving information regarding problems. This was the only method available 10–20 years ago and was extremely costly in terms of time, money and manpower for management. This is one of the reasons why management was often hesitant about implementing quality management systems inside companies.

Today computers provide the answer to this problem. The revolution that has taken place in information management systems has made this task much easier, unbelievably quicker and much more accurate. The chapter on computers discusses how to use computers in this area and which software can be used. What follows is a brief discussion of how computers perform this task.

The checksheets and control charts used to collect information can also be called *forms*. A similar form can be created on a computer with a similar appearance. The data from sheets has to be transformed to forms on computers. In a sophisticated system, with several terminals for operators to enter data into computers and sensors that pass information directly to the computers with minimum human intervention, there is no need for paper checksheets. This eliminates the need for paper completely as everything can be done directly with computers. After the information has been entered giving a command such as 'Enter' or 'Done' will store all of the information in a structure called a *table* inside the computer. Tables are similar to registers, used in offices to store various kinds of information. They contain rows and columns that store information in a form in which it can later be retrieved in convenient formats.

Information is retrieved from these tables to find and analyze the cause of the problem. The tables should be able to provide information such as the number of defects produced by each employee or the number of defects produced by each machine. Computers can also provide this information in various graph-like formats, Pareto charts and so on.

Having collected information about defective goods and organized it in computers, the next challenge will be to use this information to find out the root cause of the problem. If the list of non-conformance areas is clear and the checksheets are designed with a good understanding of the process and the information recorded in the computers correctly, then this task will not be too difficult.

7.4 IDENTIFYING ROOT CAUSES[3]

Quality management consultants have developed several tools to identify the root causes. These tools help organize and analyze information so that it is easy to trace the problem.

7.4.1 Pareto Chart

The Pareto chart orders the problems from the most to the least significant. This will help identify the most significant problems so that effort can be concentrated to get the maximum benefit at the least cost. The Pareto chart is basically a bar chart based on the principle that a few causes account for most of the problems.

The nineteenth century Italian economist, Vilfredo Pareto, first observed this now widely accepted principle when he noted that a large proportion of the national wealth was controlled by a relatively small number of people, roughly according to the ratio, 80 : 20. The Pareto principle can also be applied to quality improvement; solving a few key quality problems can lead to major improvements. Figure 7.4 shows an example of a Pareto chart.

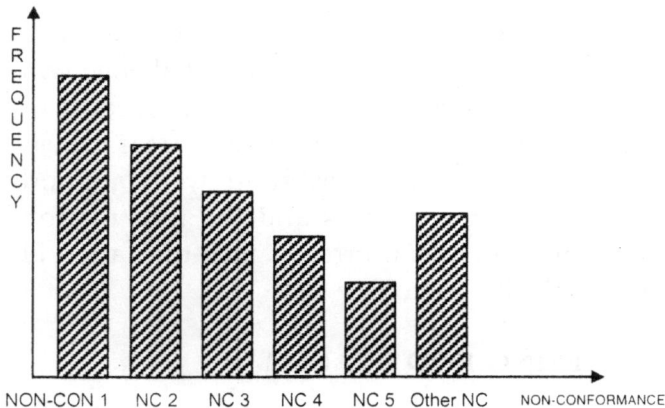

Fig. 7.4 Pareto Chart

7.4.2 Brainstorming

Brainstorming is an activity that promotes group participation and teamwork; it encourages creative thinking and stimulates the generation of as many ideas as possible in a short period of time. The participants in a brainstorming session are invited on the basis of their particular knowledge and experience and are expected to contribute to the topic under discussion. An atmosphere is created where everyone feels free to express himself or herself. The production of random or 'off the top of the head' ideas is encouraged and the emphasis is on quantity rather than quality. No criticism, expression of doubt or hasty judgement of the ideas is allowed until after the brainstorming session. This is crucial if the barriers to creative thinking—such as the fear of saying something foolish—are to be overcome.

All ideas without exception are recorded and made visible to all the participants. Each input and contribution is recognized as important and the output of the whole session is seen in context. The continuing involvement of each participant is assured and the groups' future is reinforced by mapping out the exact follow up actions—analysis and evaluation of ideas—and the future progress of the project.

7.4.3 Ishikawa Diagram

Named after Professor K. Ishikawa who introduced it, this diagram is a technique for identifying the most probable causes, after the root causes, affecting a problem. It helps in the analysis of cause and effect relationships. This diagram is also known as the fish bone diagram because of its appearance. When drawing this diagram the main problem or effect is placed in a box on the right side and a long horizontal line is drawn pointing to the box. The major categories of causes are recorded on either side of the horizontal line within boxes. These boxes are connected to the horizontal line with lines drawn at angles. Then minor cause boxes are connected to the angled lines by small horizontal lines. In this way, each main cause can be viewed as an effect in its own right with its own process line, around which other (minor) causes can be clustered.

Examples of major problem causes in a production line are methods, machines, manpower and materials. An example of an Ishikawa diagram is given in Figure 7.5.

7.4.4 Flow Chart

A flow chart is a pictorial representation of the stages in a process. Symbols, connected to each other in a

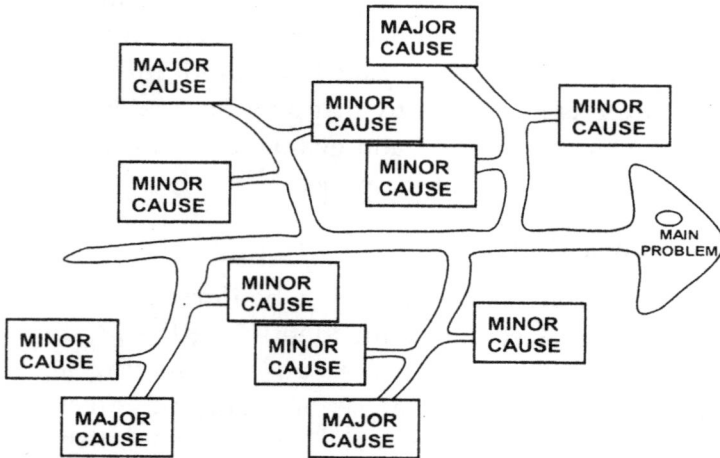

Fig. 7.5 Ishikawa Diagram

logical series, portray activities, decisions and databases, thus depicting how the process actually works. This allows complex procedure to be broken down into manageable parts for examination and better understanding. By using flow charts the problematic process areas can be identified so that quality checking can be implemented. A flow chart also shows without confusion how a process can be redesigned. Figure 7.6 shows the symbols that are used in a flow chart and a typical flow chart.

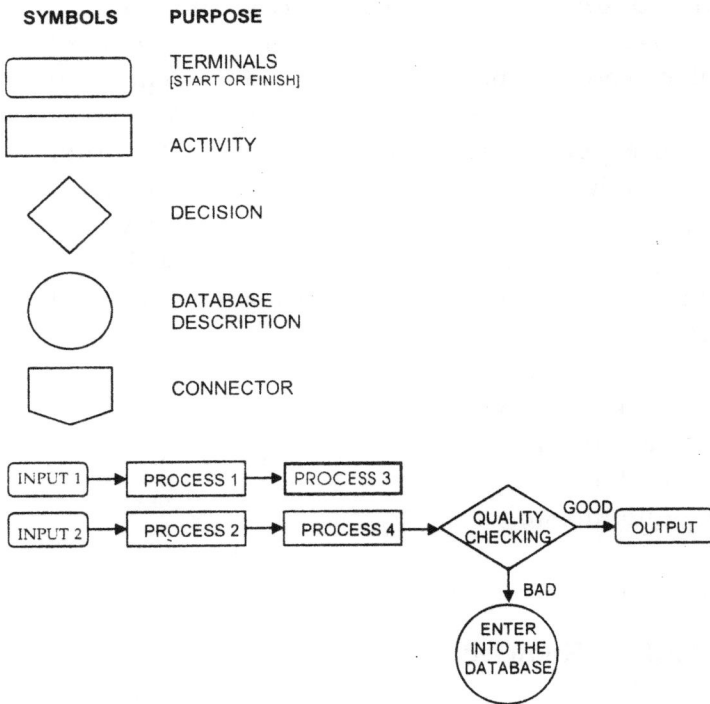

Fig. 7.6 Symbols Used in Flow Charts and a Typical Flow Chart

In addition to above tools, using software called Relational Databases to store information makes it possible to retrieve it again under specific criteria. The database can be used to retrieve information under any criteria: for example, give all information about products that have XX type of defect. The assistance of a computer programmer should be sought when setting up this type of system and this topic will be further discussed in Chapter Fourteen.

7.5 CAUSES OF DEFECTS[2]

Even though there has been a great increase in knowledge over the past few years it has still not been possible to prevent mistakes, defects and accidents from occurring in day-to-day life. Why is this? The answer has two aspects, one philosophical and the other practical. While the philosophical aspect can be safely left to the philosophers it is possible to try and understand, and thereby prevent, practical defects within organizations. There are four possible causes of defects:

1. Lack of knowledge
2. Lack of training
3. Lack of attention
4. Intentional.

Let us discuss these four areas in detail.

7.5.1 Lack of Knowledge

When a defect occurs constantly from all employees, all machines, in all environments it can be safely assumed that there is a lack of knowledge on how to prevent that particular defect. In such situations there is a need for research and experimentation to improve knowledge. The chapter on 'scientific methods' will discuss experimental research in greater detail.

7.5.2 Lack of Training

When a defect occurs only with a few employees and such employees are found to be newcomers then it can be assumed that there is a lack of training. Spending time and money on training may help solve this problem.

7.5.3 Lack of Attention

The third cause of defects may be lack of attention. It is the major cause of accidents. Lack of attention may be the result of too much work or fatigue. Frequent breaks or making work more varied and interesting for employees by rotating jobs may help prevent defects caused by lack of attention.

7.5.4 Intentional

Finally, it is also possible that some defects are caused by intentional action. When an individual or group of employees who were once working hard and producing good quality products suddenly start producing defects, the likely cause is intentional action. When fatigue and other similar causes have been ruled out, intentional action remains the only likely cause.

Even though such situations are disappointing and irritating for a manager, they have to be borne patiently. Such employees initially came to the organization with the intention of working hard and have previously had a very good working record. What could be the sudden cause of the problem? It may be a supervisor or uncomfortable conditions in the working environment. There are two choices facing the manager: either reprimanding the employees without dealing with the cause or removing the cause so that employees can resume their former working efficiency. The choice depends on how good a strategic thinker the manager is.

We have so far discussed how to identify customer dissatisfaction, translate dissatisfaction into a technical language, record non-conformance and analyze non-conformance data to find the root causes of problems. It is now possible to discuss necessary corrective action. Before that, however, it is useful to discuss some other associated factors that will not only help implement corrective action but also help identify defects, causes of defects and their possible solutions. The factors are the development of a company-wide communication system, understanding employee expectations and developing a training program to implement quality.

This chapter does not contain a section on the service sector as all the techniques and tools discussed above can be equally and efficiently used to identify problems in the service sector as well. Usually the root causes are more difficult to identify in the service sector. The administration in the service sector can use these tools to identify the root causes in their areas.

Chapter Eight

Developing a Communication System for TQM

8.1 IMPORTANCE OF COMMUNICATION

Quality management is an information-related management system. An efficient communication system is an important requirement for the functioning of quality management systems.

Quality management requires the communication of different types of information: information about customer complaints that must be transferred to the appropriate department for necessary corrective action and feedback information about defective goods in each department. It is also important to communicate with employees about the progress of quality management and the corrective actions that are being taken. Basically, when a quality management system is being implemented, it is important to communicate with everybody so that all employees are kept informed about the changes going around.

A communication system is also important in developing a common language inside the company to break down the barriers of fear that block the path towards quality improvement.

8.2 A COMMON LANGUAGE FOR THE COMPANY

In quality management one of the important issues that is discussed from different perspectives is the use of slogans. There are two different ideas regarding the use of slogans. On one side, it is argued that slogans develop a common language that motivates employees while the other view rejects slogans as an unnecessary irritation for employees that causes fear and conflicts between employees. It is possible to solve this problem through the human body example that was discussed in Chapter Four.

8.2.1 The Uniform Identity of the Human Body

There are millions of cells within the body. There is a great variety amongst them in terms of type, function and life span. Whatever the cell type, the body's immune system is able to identify them and does not attack them as being foreign. But when a different type of cells enter the body, for example bacterial cells or cells from another human in the form of a tissue transplant, the body immediately identifies them and attempts to destroy them. The only exception would be cells from identical twins. It is not necessary to consider the complicated cell biology of this process here but it is possible to use some of the basic concepts.

Most of the cells in the body have a single identity displayed on the cell membrane. As long as the cells have this identity the immune cells will take no action. Conflict occurs when immune cells come across a cell without the appropriate identification. How can a similar system be implemented inside organizations and companies? What can bring about this unique identity recognition between employees?

What is needed is a common identity. It need not be a long sentence that includes all quality management concepts or some words that simply try and irritate the workers into doing something. It can be a simple logo or simple slogan that every institution has. The important point here is that such identification should be acceptable to everybody working inside the organization and should accept the superiority of quality and the importance of the customer.

In a multiethnic or multi-religion society where such slogans are not acceptable for a particular group, it becomes the cause of problems. What is needed is a change, which assures that all employees use the logo. It may be a uniform, T-shirt, badge and so on. Common violations of such rules usually do not come from the lower levels but from upper-level management and professionals. The important thing to remember is that when not wearing the logo is a sign of superiority, it produces disrespect for the logo amongst employees at all levels. It leads to an identification of division between employees and further conflict.

8.2.2 Cancers of the Organization

What is the cause of cancer? Sometimes cells inside body undergo some changes and start to take in a lot of food and divide rapidly and even start to kill normal cells. The important thing here is that these cells do not lose the identity of the normal cells so that the immune cells cannot identify the cancerous cells and remove them.

Corrupt people inside organizations behave in the same way as cancerous cells. They waste the resources of the organization. They spread their mentality rapidly inside the organization. They often hold on strongly to the identity of the organization in order to protect themselves. Commonly, these people are found to be good friends of upper management so that no corrective actions can be taken against them. As surgery is the only solution for cancer, so when a system gets corrupted, tough actions are necessary to solve problems inside the company. Usually such tough action can be only taken by people coming from outside.

8.3 BREAKING THE BARRIERS[3]

Another important function of a communication system is to break barriers between departments and individuals and dispel the fear surrounding quality management procedures. The management style of standing in front of all employees and giving instructions in a high tone should be avoided. This management style may be useful in emergency cases but it is not the way of quality management. In quality management, workers should be consulted individually or in small teams so that two-way communication is achieved. Encouraging employees to discuss their personal goals will help achieve a good rapport and create a secure environment.

Some managers prefer to create a climate of fear. They believe that they will appear more important if their employees are afraid of them. They also believe that workers will perform better if they are insecure or anxious about their jobs. But the actual result of such practices is stress, demotivation, work being done wrong deliberately, fiddling of figures, time wasted in looking and applying for other jobs and valuable **personnel** being lost, usually to competitors. In such circumstances, important information about defects is lost in an attempt to bury the evidence.

Today's managers have to accept that the days when managers were responsible for thinking and workers for implementing have now long passed. A company trying to survive on the intelligence of only a handful of managers has no chance of surviving in the new economic age. A mobilization of every bit of all employees' intelligence is needed for survival. The breaking down of barriers through adequate communication can achieve this mobilization. Managers have to face up to a new philosophy of pulling together the intellectual resources of all employees for the benefit of the company. Lack of proper communication inhibits the development and implementation of innovative ideas, which remain just ideas.

The important fact that has to be accepted is that quality cannot be achieved when inputs are of low quality, machines are not fit, working conditions are poor and employees' benefits are removed to make profits. In such situations no employee will accept the company's identity and goals as his own. A worker can function only as long as the system allows. Beyond this, it is the responsibility of management to ensure that the worker is motivated and not handicapped by the system.

At this point, it is useful to introduce another example from the human body. As previously discussed, the body is made up of millions of cells of a multitude of functions. Inside the body every cell has certain functions and for some functional reasons each cell has to be placed in a particular part of the body. For example a red blood cell can travel through the entire body but not into the spinal canal. This does not mean that the red blood cell is a second-class citizen inside the body. Basically every single cell inside the body is provided with all the information needed to build another body and thus there are no secrets between two different cells inside the body, even if they have different functions. Even red blood cells that have a life span of only 120 days and no nucleus, contain all the necessary information to build another human body. This is what the film "Jurassic Park" is all about.

8.4 COMMUNICATION SYSTEM FOR THE COMPANY

With the above understanding of the importance of communication, it is now possible to try and develop a communication system for an organization or company. It is important to divide the organization into manageable units so that we can implement a communication system for efficient function.

Section 6.3 discussed methods of developing a quality management skeleton for the organization. There it was seen that certain departments could be considered a unit for quality management system implementation. What should be the average size of a department? In a university the usual size of a department might be 15–25 people but in the automobile industry the departmental size could be 500 people. For the purposes of communication such a large size may be an acceptable unit for some kind of information but for some other purpose it may be necessary to divide the department into smaller units. Before turning to what size is acceptable for which purpose, a brief discussion of the issues that need to be communicated inside the company would be in order.

Inside the department it is necessary to communicate four different types of information.

1. General information, information about events inside the department, company and community events such as the birthdays of workers.
2. Information about present quality level, the abstracted and summarized information from the checklist.
3. Information about success stories and appreciation.
4. Information about innovation, contribution to quality improvement and corrective action.

For the first three kinds of information the usual department size may be a convenient size for communication. We can use display boards for such purposes. Figure 8.1 gives an idea of a display board.

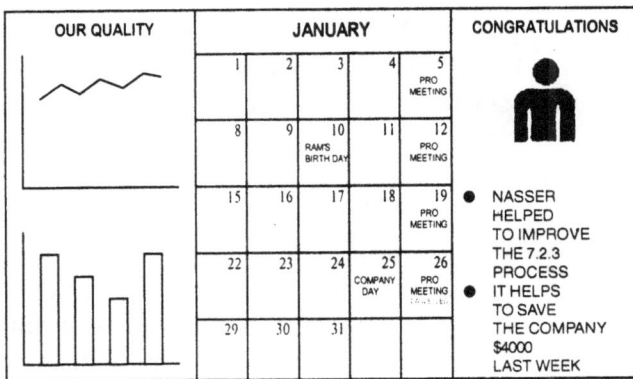

OUR QUALITY	JANUARY					CONGRATULATIONS
	1	2	3	4	5 PRO MEETING	
	8	9	10 RAM'S BIRTH DAY	11	12 PRO MEETING	
	15	16	17	18	19 PRO MEETING	● NASSER HELPED TO IMPROVE THE 7.2.3 PROCESS
	22	23	24	25 COMPANY DAY	26 PRO MEETING	● IT HELPS TO SAVE
	29	30	31			THE COMPANY $4000 LAST WEEK

Fig. 8.1 Display Board for Internal Communication

A much smaller sized unit is needed when communicating information about innovation and corrective action so that everyone can give his or her suggestions and be heard by other members of the group. For such meetings the optimum size might be 10–15 people. When the numbers get above 20 the unit should be split into two smaller groups. How should the department be organized into smaller groups?

People working in a particular type of workstation could be grouped together. Such places are ideal for brainstorming activity. Meetings should be scheduled for the beginning or middle of the day. Trying to hold such a meeting in the last few hours when employees are thinking of going home won't help. In such places free communication should be encouraged so that constructive ideas will be produced. The things that need to be discussed include the quality of the worksite, improvements to working conditions and so on.

The three important people who need to be present in all such meetings are the manager of the department, manager for quality control and the technical person in charge of the department. Without the presence of these people the meetings will not be successful in trying to find immediate solutions. All the suggestions in such areas should be documented through a proper suggestion system for the worksite.

Besides establishing formal communication channels, management should also go to the grass roots to establish informal communication channels with all employees. In such places trying to communicate about the quality of production may give a negative result. Instead, it may be better to talk to employees about personal goals and improving working conditions. These issues will be discussed in further detail in Chapter Nine, when we talk about, 'Management by Walking Around'.

8.5 SUGGESTION SYSTEM

It has been established that in quality management it is important to mobilize the intelligence of all employees in order to produce a company-wide innovation ethics. Other than the fear created by some managers, another factor that prevents some employees' coming forward with their ideas is suspicion about the management's fairness. When some useful ideas come from bottom-line workers, the usual person who brings it to the attention of upper management is either the department manager or the engineer. The usual result is that the name of the actual person who gave the idea is forgotten or hidden and the manager or engineer gets the credit. What results from this is a bitter experience that keeps employees away from production improvement programs and brainstorming activities.

So what the upper management has to do here is to ensure that a well-documented suggestion system is placed throughout the company, which should be administered by the upper management. It is important to ensure that all suggestions whether they come during review meetings or individual suggestions get entered into such documents. For best results, information from such documents should be entered into a computerized database management system for better organization.

A suggestion identification number should be given to employees, with ways and rights to know what happened to the suggestion. A sample form for such suggestion is show in Figure 8.2.

XXXXX COMPANY
SUGGESTION FORM

COMPANY WILL ALWAYS WELCOME AND WILL APPRECIATE YOUR USEFUL IDEAS TO IMPROVE THE PRODUCTION

NEED TO BE FILLED BY THE MANAGEMENT

SUGGESTION ID NO [ ] RELEVANT PRODUCTION PROCESS CONTROL MANUAL NO [ ]

RECEIVED BY [ ] Signature [ ]

FILLED BY EMPLOYEE

DEPARTMENT NAME [ ] RELEVANT PRODUCTION PROCESS CONTROL MANUAL NO [ ]

EMPLOYEE NAME [ ] EMP ID [ ]

PRESENT PROCEDURE

YOUR SUGGESTION

- -

ACKNOWLEDGEMENT CARD (SUGGESTION FORM)

TO:-..

I confirm you that I have received your suggestion regarding

....

....

ID No for Suggestion [ ]

MANAGER [ ] Signature [ ]

Fig. 8.2 Sample Suggestion Form

On the back of the acknowledgements section of the suggestion form, the following information can be printed:

If you would like to know about what happened to your suggestion feel free to communicate with your manager or section engineer. Using the ID number of your suggestion, you can get an immediate reply from administration regarding the position of your suggestion.

Such a form should be made freely available to all employees and it is the responsibility of the management to record any suggestion that is received in production review meetings or in any other situation. When a decision is made regarding the suggestion the employee should be informed.

8.6 COMMUNICATION IN THE SERVICE SECTOR

Although the service sector faces unique problems, a lot of improvement can be achieved by computerizing communication system in the services. As previously discussed, the service sector uses a lot of indices for its functions. Before the computer age, preparing an annual report about these indices often involved waiting for a year. This meant that the annual report for 1998 would only have been available in 2000. Using a computerized information management system it is possible to make such a report within a month, that is in February 1999. Another important difference between communication in the service and manufacturing sector is in cooperating with customers to plan corrective action. Especially in the education or public services if improvement ideas are formulated in cooperation with students and service users, such improvements can often be implemented with greater success.

Chapter Nine

TOWARDS A BETTER UNDERSTANDING OF EMPLOYEES

9.1 MOTIVATING THE EMPLOYEES

One of the most challenging questions facing every manager is how to motivate the employees. One of the most frequent answers to the question is that there are no constant factors that work beyond a certain period of time. Several philosophies have been elaborated and several studies have been conducted to answer the above question. Let us focus on one particular study that will provide a deep understanding of the issues surrounding employee morale.

9.1.1 Hawthorne Experiments[16]

These studies were conducted by the Harvard Business School at the Hawthorne plant in Illinois, USA. The research was conducted from 1924 to 1932 and the reports were published over a period of approximately 10 years thereafter. The studies were known as the Hawthorne Research or the Hawthorne Experiments. The researchers were trying to identify factors responsible for the motivation of employees. Many factors were investigated—for example, what effect lighting might have on employee productivity.

The researchers increased the level of lighting in an experimental room and found that productivity increased, but when the level of lighting was reduced, the productivity was again found to increase. An increase in productivity was also noted in a control room where lighting was not altered. In another experiment, despite various changes, it was found that productivity remained low and constant.

The experiments were undertaken at a time when the idea of individuality remained supreme in industry; the ideas of Adam Smith had firmly taken root. The worker was viewed as an economic man selling his individual labour at the best possible price he could secure as a competitive individual. His objective was the profit motive and it was believed that most of his energies were directed towards this objective.

However, the Hawthorne experiments seemed to show the importance of social and human elements in the behaviour of individual workers. The investigators noticed the development of a new 'social situation' during the course of the experiment. They noticed the formation of informal groups or 'cliques'. These cliques worked according to the working conditions, when they thought that the conditions were favourable to them they worked hard to maintain them. In other instances, when a clique thought that working slowly would provide job security, no inducement could make them work faster. From these experiments, the following facts can be discerned: positive team spirit can only bring better productivity; work security is important in establishing good productivity; good productivity requires a good team leader.

9.1.2 Maslows' Need Hierarchy

Maslows' need hierarchy can be used to provide an explanation of human needs and how these are satisfied inside organizations. Whilst managers think that employees get paid for their work, it is important to consider why employees come to work. They come to work to satisfy some needs and achieve certain goals. When managing people, it is important to try and understand what employees' goals and needs are. A successful manager will help employees satisfy their needs and help them to achieve their goals. Figure 9.1 shows Maslows' Need Hierarchy that will help understand employees' goals and needs and how to satisfy them.

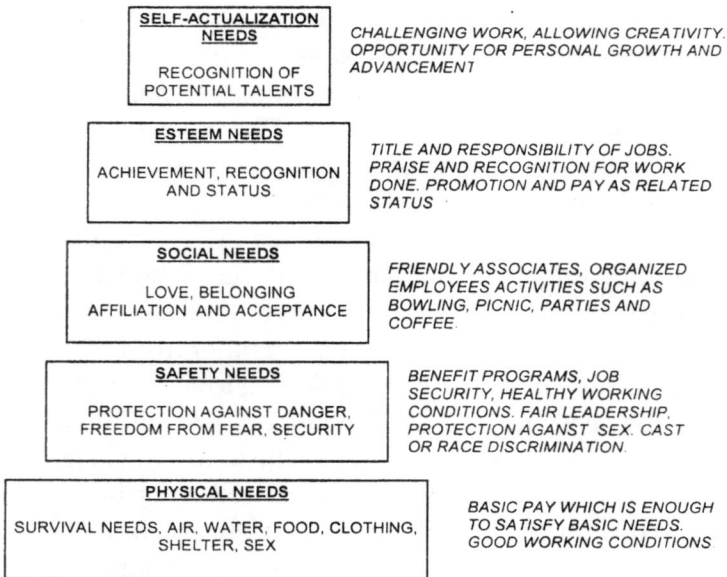

SELF-ACTUALIZATION NEEDS RECOGNITION OF POTENTIAL TALENTS	*CHALLENGING WORK, ALLOWING CREATIVITY. OPPORTUNITY FOR PERSONAL GROWTH AND ADVANCEMENT*
ESTEEM NEEDS ACHIEVEMENT, RECOGNITION AND STATUS	*TITLE AND RESPONSIBILITY OF JOBS. PRAISE AND RECOGNITION FOR WORK DONE. PROMOTION AND PAY AS RELATED STATUS*
SOCIAL NEEDS LOVE, BELONGING AFFILIATION AND ACCEPTANCE	*FRIENDLY ASSOCIATES, ORGANIZED EMPLOYEES ACTIVITIES SUCH AS BOWLING, PICNIC, PARTIES AND COFFEE.*
SAFETY NEEDS PROTECTION AGAINST DANGER, FREEDOM FROM FEAR, SECURITY	*BENEFIT PROGRAMS, JOB SECURITY, HEALTHY WORKING CONDITIONS. FAIR LEADERSHIP, PROTECTION AGANST SEX. CAST OR RACE DISCRIMINATION.*
PHYSICAL NEEDS SURVIVAL NEEDS, AIR, WATER, FOOD, CLOTHING, SHELTER, SEX	*BASIC PAY WHICH IS ENOUGH TO SATISFY BASIC NEEDS. GOOD WORKING CONDITIONS*

Fig. 9.1 Maslows' Need Hierarchy and Ways to Satisfy Them.
Motivation and Personality 3/E by Maslow, © Reprinted by permission of Pearson Education, Inc., Upper Saddle River, JN.

A common mistake done here is trying to satisfy one of the upper needs without satisfying the lower ones. An example is a Black American Olympic gold winner who threw his gold medal into a river when he got racially discriminated. This may be an extreme example. A more common management experience might be trying to organize a social gathering without adequate pay and fair leadership; attendance will be poor and participation will be reluctant. Employees will see attempts to satisfy higher needs without satisfying lower ones as an attempt to cheat them.

9.1.3 Motivation in TQM

Quality management professionals agree that an important aspect of motivating employees is appreciating their work. There is, however, disagreement as to how to identify well-performing employees within the organization.

In Deming's view meriting individual employees can lead to personal disappointment and disillusion. He argues that annual merit ratings can cause excessive internal conflict and isolation as well as reducing risk-taking and initiative. If the traditional idea of rating employees from first to last has to be abandoned, what is the best way of selecting employees for appreciation? Section 8.5 discussed the idea of a suggestion system. It is not possible to build a complete suggestion system without appreciating useful ideas received. Appreciation for a suggestion can take the form that the employee would find useful, perhaps even a scholarship for studies. The award can be given at an employee gathering with a chance for the employee concerned to speak about the suggestion.

Crosby discusses the issues related to selecting an employee who has been producing good quality. He suggests that a person could be selected through a mini-democratic system within the company. Employees could suggest a name other than their own for a quality prize. The names of management and professional people have to be avoided for such a system. Selecting individuals through this procedure can help avoid isolation following appreciation ceremonies and also help develop a positive habit of appreciating co-workers within a team.

9.2 SOLVING EMPLOYEES' PROBLEMS[16]

It has been suggested that employees come to work to satisfy their needs and goals and that a good management will help employees achieve these aims with minimum disturbance to the production system. This may involve giving employees special leave for an examination or advance payment for some personal reason. Today's factory system of production means that employees are more likely to face certain specific problems than these common problems. A good understanding of these problems and ways to solve them is important for a manager and for his or her efficient functioning. What follows is a discussion of some of these problems in greater detail.

9.2.1 Factory System of Production

The industrial revolution was brought about by several factors. Alongside the social, economic and political factors, is the system of factory production. The factory system of production involves a number of processes.

Among them division of labour, specialization, mechanization, reutilization and automation are the important ones.

- **Division of Labour and Specialization**

  The division of labour is a process of simplification, whereby a single task is broken up into a whole series of smaller tasks that are simpler and more specialized. Adam Smith famously divided the task of manufacturing a pin into a series of 18 steps. Specialization is the result of a division of labour as each individual performs only the task that is expected of him or her. The individual learns the skills of his or her particular operation thoroughly. Consequent upon the improvement of the skills of the operatives, the operations become specialized and total output increases. A study from the United States suggests that due to specialization the average output has seen a six-fold increase in the past century.

  Although division of labour and specialization have increased production there are some associated problems with these processes. The first is that the repetitive performance of the same operation becomes monotonous for the operatives. Specialization in just one sequence means that employees lose the chance of becoming familiar with the whole activity. Ignorance of the entire process can lead to alienation and disturbances amongst personnel. The division of labour not only divides jobs, it also divides people. As Ruskin says, "It is not the labour that is divided but the men." Because of the division of labour the idea of a society with 'integrated, combined labour' cannot be achieved. It may lead to a lack of solidarity and the possibility of discontent within society.

- **Mechanization**

A machine is a device that indirectly performs some task without human intervention. The duty of men is to tend, feed, operate and generally look after the running of the machine using sources of energy such as electricity or petroleum. The machine took a firm grip on industry during the industrial revolution that took place in England in the latter half of the 18th century. It appeared first in the textile industry and then spread to other industries.

The machine produces some effects on the psychology of men engaged in the productive process. The machine tends to reduce the worker to an appendage of itself, destroying the need for skill. As a result, the worker becomes exposed to the danger of monotony and boredom. Workers are often dominated by a sense of the meaninglessness of work and by a lack of interest in the job. More importantly machines cause a profound feeling of insecurity in the worker.

- **Routinization**

Machines have routinized the process of production to an extreme degree. The worker has been turned into an automation, a mere robot performing a task in a never changing fashion. The machine has not only reduced man to an accessory in the system of production and an extension of itself, it has also made man into a machine. This can lead to psychological problems for individuals.

- **Automation**

  Automation involves two things: first, under a system of automation material is handled and transferred automatically without any activity from humans; second, a system of automation involves a process whereby information on the state of the work cycle is fed to some central agency which then feeds back orders or correction to the work process. This central agency, usually an electronic device, then directs the machine to make adjustments, that channel, the work process in the desired direction. Thus automation takes over not only motor tasks from humans but also performs some sensory tasks that were previously thought to be only capable of being performed by men. While automation produces increased production with low manpower, it leads to mass unemployment. This is alongside other effects on the personality such as, fatigue and boredom as well as a sense of job insecurity.

9.2.2 Solving the Problem

As discussed, although the factory system is efficient, it imposes certain strains on the role of the worker. Unfortunately there is no more efficient system than the factory system. Therefore the problems within the factory system have to be solved for more efficient function. Let us discuss how these problems can be solved within organizations.

- **Rest Phase**

  The first proposal that has been made to alleviate the monotony and boredom of industrialized work is the rest phase. The rest phase reduces monotony by releasing the worker from the routine of the task. It gives the worker a chance to establish social contacts with other workers and establish or renew friendships that vary experience. It has been suggested that 10 or 15 minute rest phases, duly administered during the work hours, can be very effective in reducing monotony.

- **Changes in the Method of Work**

  Sometimes boredom in the job can be reduced by changing the methods of work or by shifting jobs. The effectiveness of this method lies in the breaking the routine of work and in the change that enables the worker to employ and learn some different skills.

- **Method of Payment**

  It is sometimes held that adopting a suitable method of payment can counteract boredom. Usually this means piece rate payment or some other sort of financial incentive, such as a bonus plan. The theory behind this method is that the worker will become so absorbed in meeting a certain goal of production that he or she will come to feel that there is a meaning to the job and a positive reason for work. However, this method has been shown empirically to be of limited value; the financial incentive is distant and does not change the nature of work itself.

- **Working in Compact Social Groups**

  Another proposal is that production could be carried out in compact social groups that will permit certain types of social relationship, for example, exchange of conversation that does not interfere with production. According to this point of view, monotony will be reduced or eliminated as the worker finds alternative expressive outlets. However, it must be kept in mind that informal social groups are not the panacea for all the ills of industry. Certain informal groups may serve as instruments of additional construction for the individual worker than as outlets for psychological needs.

- **Training Programs for New Techniques**

  Whenever some new technique is introduced inside an organization, instead of laying off all of the old workers and hiring new people, training programs can be introduced internally or externally to train the existing workers. This will not only increase job security but will also ensure that experienced workers are not lost from the company.

  The strains produced on the worker by the factory system of production can be overcome by applying appropriate techniques and efficient management. When planning the worksite, it is important not to make things too mechanical or repetitive. By introducing rest phases and job rotation, the major problems of factory production can be overcome.

9.3 UNDERSTANDING EMPLOYEES' CAPABILITIES

Management failure to understand and appreciate employee talents is often a greater cause for dissatisfaction amongst employees. Every employee is an individual with a distinct personality, goals and abilities to perform different tasks. It is the responsibility of management to understand the differences between individuals and organize workers in a way that is best suited to utilizing their talents and realizing their goals. Deming, in his discussion on training, emphasizes the importance of teaching psychology to managers so that they can better understand their employees. Here a brief discussion of employees' capabilities and skills would be in order.

An individual's capabilities can be divided into two categories: physical capabilities and mental capabilities. Physical capabilities are the ability of the individual to do physical work. Work that involves lifting heavy objects requires a steady muscular frame while minute intricate work requires someone with fine finger movements and good hand to eye coordination.

Mental capabilities can be divided into three groups: personal knowledge; intelligence and finally personality.

9.3.1 Individual Knowledge

The process of learning is continuous from birth to death. An individual's knowledge comes from education and experience and from various people and places. There are two different categories of work-related knowledge. The first is whether the individual is capable of performing the job and the second is whether the individual has wider knowledge of how the task is related to other issues outside the field. Both types of knowledge are important in performing a job efficiently. While specific knowledge may be adequate for technicians and those below that level, at higher levels, professionals and administrative individuals require wider knowledge to perform their task well.

It is important to remember that divisions between different types of knowledge have been made for our ease but in reality there is a great deal of overlap between the different fields. Knowledge can be tested through a number of mechanisms that include paper-based examinations and long interviews. Each mechanism has its advantages and disadvantages. In today's world there is a lot to learn and it is difficult to keep everything in the memory, so paper-based exams and interviews cannot be considered appropriate methods of testing an individual's knowledge. A more appropriate method might be to check an individual's ability to gather information on a particular problem using a library or the Internet and to suggest a solution to the problem on that basis.

9.3.2 Intelligence

Intelligence can be defined as an individual's ability to understand problems and find solutions. Even if an individual has very good knowledge, intelligence is key to understanding problems and applying appropriate knowledge. Unlike knowledge, which can be acquired from education and experience, intelligence is more or less determined at birth. Which factors are responsible for determining intelligence? There is a big list of possible suggestions but no definitive answers. It is generally accepted that a healthy pregnancy with a healthy birth, good nutrition from a young age and certain genetic factors account for good intelligence. Similarly, problems with pregnancy or childbirth, poor nutrition and diseases affecting the brain are thought to be responsible for poor intelligence.

The important point to remember is that there are no differences in the distribution of intelligence between different countries or races. Some earlier studies suggested some differences but this was later found to be caused by bias in the way tests were conducted. Although some societies are considered more intelligent than others, this is probably due to better educational facilities, greater opportunities to bring out hidden intelligence and more respect for intelligence than in other societies. Techniques that appear to improve performance in intelligence tests actually just provide a mechanism of familiarization with the exam process and allow the expression of hidden intelligence rather than increase intelligence. It should be noted that while there are no drugs that can improve intelligence, several drugs could actually impair intelligence.

Although it is not possible to increase innate intelligence, constant education and involvement in problem-solving activities will help maintain intelligence. Intelligence examinations are generally conducted to screen a large number of employees for a particular job.

9.3.3 Personality

Personality can be defined as the way an individual responds to different situations. Each individual will respond in a different way. It is generally accepted that personality is moulded during childhood and teenage years and stays throughout adulthood without much modification. Psychiatrists often attempt to change an individual's personality when it causes a problem to the individual or to the society at large. Such attempts usually take a great deal of time and even though there may be some success stories, there are many failures.

The best way to deal with different personalities is to find a job that will suit each person and his or her personality. Some personalities are more suited to clerical work while others are better suited for scientific jobs. It is the responsibility of the management to find which personality is suited for which job and then accommodate everyone in the most practicable way.

Using the above discussion on individual physical and mental ability it should be possible to understand employees' talents and organize them in the most efficient and appropriate way for the company. A variety of differences between individuals should be regarded as an asset that can be utilized rather than as an inhibitory factor. The diverse abilities of individuals should be identified and utilized in a manner beneficial for the company.

9.4 TEAM AND MODERN LEADERSHIP

One of the most important findings of the Hawthorne experiments was that a positive team spirit could help increase production. How can team spirit be developed and under what conditions can it be achieved? To establish a positive team spirit, it is important to provide an environment that is free of fear in which all employees can take pride in their work, feel respected and accepted, feel as if they are part of a team and in which they can strive not only for their own interest but for the interest of the whole organization. Proper working conditions, adequate education and training, good communication and cooperation, a modern leadership, good material and equipment, appropriate quality tools and job satisfaction lie at the basis of eliminating fear and building a good team environment.

The most important factor that prevents the creation of a good team spirit is job insecurity. This is another important finding of the Hawthorne experiment. It is observed that workers tried to restrict production when they felt threatened by job insecurity. Workers know from experience that their tenure on the job is related to the flow of manufacturing and they try and increase their tenure by 'stretching out the work'. The workers reason, rightly or not, that by working rapidly and efficiently they may increase the income for a while but face an earlier lay off. The workers reasoning may appear fallacious but they are judging on the basis of their experience and this tells them that if they slow down the pace of their work, there will be more work; that if they work too fast, their job may be in danger.

Although quality management is a highly decentralized system that depends on the intelligence and cooperation of all employees, the leadership role is not fully eliminated. Instead the leadership role has become more important and challenging, as it has changed from the old hierarchical watchdog style supervision to the modern information-guided, people-orientated management system. The leaders that are needed today are not overseers or judges but counsellors and teachers. Leaders should work with people, trying to identify their problems and improving the system in which they work. They should be supportive, sympathetic, encouraging and helpful to all employees in solving employee problems at work and in the achievement of their personal goals.

Leadership and supervision should concentrate on making workers take more interest in their work. An interested worker will want to do the job well and will accept advice, training and help for doing it in the best possible way. When implementing a quality management system inside the company, it is the responsibility of top management to create a company-wide quality policy, demonstrate commitment to it and create a system appropriate for a TQM culture. It is the responsibility of middle management to ensure that TQM principles are communicated and spread adequately throughout the company so that a TQM culture is maintained and eventually brings results. One of the most important functions of management in this regard is the mobilization of all the intelligence of employees. This is achieved by breaking down barriers and eliminating fear through adequate communication. Top managers have to face up to a new philosophy of pulling together the intellectual resources of all employees for the benefit of the company.

An important topic of discussion in quality management is MBWA (management by walking around or wandering around). The efficiency of this technique depends on what goal is being sought by walking around the worksite. If MBWA is used to identify defects and the causes of defects in order to give on-site corrective instructions to employees, it is just the old style of watchdog administration under a new name. If a computer-based complete information management system has been installed in the company, then it is possible to find out defects and the causes of defects by sitting in front of the computer. However, in MBWA the manager can use worksite visits to learn from employees what obstacles they face and their personal goals. The manager should communicate with the employees on methods to overcome obstacles and achieve ambitions. It is more useful if the manager behaves as a counsellor and friend rather than supervisor or overseer.

9.5 EMPLOYEES IN THE SERVICE SECTOR

All the information that has been discussed so far is important and essential for employees in the service sector as well. Democratic and decentralized procedures are also more important in the service sector, especially in fields such as medicine and education where employees can be more educated than management. Workers in service sectors also come into direct contact with customers and therefore assistance should be given to all employees on how to understand customer behaviour and establish good customer relationships.

Chapter Ten

TRAINING AND EDUCATION FOR QUALITY IMPROVEMENT

10.1 IMPORTANCE OF TRAINING

All quality management professionals agree that training and education are important in the quality improvement process. As previously discussed, quality management is a new culture and a new way of thinking, so without education and training such changes of culture cannot be achieved. Managers and other professionals have to be educated in quality management objectives and tools so that they can develop good control over them. More importantly, all other employees inside the company have to be educated to understand the importance of quality, customer satisfaction and be helped to develop some understanding of quality management tools. This understanding is important as it will help dispel the fear that is produced when the quality management process is being implemented. Quality management is an information-based management system and only education and training can provide employees with the necessary information.

When discussing training, it is important to remember that this includes retraining. Although the brain has the power of memory, it also has the weakness of forgetting; so it is important that all employees receive periodic retraining. This is specially important in certain sectors, such as medicine and technology where there is a rapid expansion of knowledge. New technologies and new methods are constantly being produced; reeducation and retraining are the only ways to maintain market position. Training does not have to be restricted to training in knowledge and skills. People working in services such as the police or fire brigade should receive regular physical training and periodic physical checkups. In Japan mild exercise in the early morning is considered beneficial for all employees. It is worth remembering that quality production has been most fully developed in Japan.

The cost of training is usually the most important factor that hinders the implementation of a training program. Training and retraining are large costs in the annual budget. The important fact that has to be remembered is that the cost of mistakes that arise out of inadequate training will usually be far greater than the cost of training itself. If employees do not have a sound and updated knowledge of their field, they will not be able to produce good quality products or services.

10.2 THE PSYCHOLOGY OF TRAINING[10]

There are a number of different schools of thought that have sought to explain the learning or training process. Educational psychologists have defined learning as a relatively permanent change in behaviour that can be explained in terms of experience or practice. In practical management of industry or services it may be more useful to think of training or learning as a way of instituting the transference of knowledge or skills to a new employee. A successful training program should first select the appropriate people. Chapter Nine discussed the psychology of individual capabilities. The usual methods used by agencies to select employees are IQ tests and skills tests.

A good training program should include ideas about people's learning behaviour. A more practical method than psychology to understand learning behaviour would be to use the following two questions.

- **The first question is: Why do people want to learn?**

There are several answers to this: they want to make money; they are afraid of losing their jobs; they want self-satisfaction—the list may extend further. It is possible to group all of the motivations into the following three:

- Desire for reward
- Self-satisfaction
- Social pressure

Despite intelligence, culture, dignity and so on, we are all motivated by one or the other reward or punishment systems. The most common motivation for learning is the need to get a good job with a good salary. The other side of the argument is also true; we want to learn for the fear of being punished if we do not.

The second reason for learning is self-satisfaction. Learning a sport or art is a way of gaining self-satisfaction. In these instance money is not the prime motivation. Sports, such as golf, cost a lot of money but are not necessarily related to work.

The final reason for any learning is social pressure. Many of our decisions, in terms of educational interests, are selected not by our own interest, but because of pressure from parents, friends and other people in our social circle. While this may not be the best way to make decisions, we have to understand that we are social animals and many of our activities are directly or indirectly regulated by our society.

- **The second question would be: Why some people do not or do not want to learn?**

  There are four main answers for this:

  - Lack of motivation
  - Lack of background
  - Rebellion against authority
  - Failure to relate training to the job.

Although the most important reason that people do not want to learn is that they are not motivated, motivation alone does not provide a complete satisfactory solution. There are other reasons why employees may not have an interest in learning, even after the advantages of learning have been pointed out to them. Sometimes the fault lies with the trainer. Most employees will not be interested in training if it is carried out in the very last part of the day. The fault may lie with the trainer who may not know how to train people or be inadequately trained and motivated.

The second reason for poor learning might be an inappropriate background. Chapter Nine discussed employee capabilities. Care should be taken during the recruitment process to ensure that the appropriate employees are selected. The recruitment process should select people who can understand the technical language that is used in the company and can acquire the necessary skills and knowledge.

The third reason that some people do not want to learn is an inherent tendency to rebel that exists in all of us. In severe cases, it is expressed in the attitude: 'You represent the management so train me, if you think you can, but you won't get any help from me.' Most of the time, it is not that bad, but we need to realize that problem can and does exit. This problem can be overcome by including enthusiasm and interest as the part of the training program. It is important to remember that not all employees are hungry for training. If they respect the company, they respect being trained. If they are not motivated to do the job, they will not be motivated by the training as well. If they feel that the company will get all benefits of their training and they will get none, they will rebel against the idea of learning more about the job.

The final reason that employees often do not want to learn is that they do not see any connection between what they are supposed to learn and what they will do when the training is over. This problem can be overcome by ensuring that the training program is directly related to the job, not only in the content, but also in the way that it looks and feels.

The above discussion on why people learn and why people do not learn can help in the understanding of the human psychology and behaviour. This knowledge not only helps in the design of a training program, but also helps solve problems that might be encountered in the training program. Let us now discuss some training tools which are crucial to developing training programs.

10.3 TRAINING TOOLS[12]

The techniques and tools of training and education have come a long way from the traditional methods of blackboard and chalk. A good understanding of these tools and techniques is important in developing a successful training program. The basis of using training tools is to achieve multiple-sense learning. Multiple-sense learning means that the same message is sent through different sensory organs like the ears and eyes. Training tools also help us explain complicated relationships between many different objects. The following training tools can be used in training programs whenever necessary.

10.3.1 Board and Board Works

There are three kinds of boards. The first one is the chalkboard, the familiar blackboards of schools days. They are of green or black matt finish and different colour chalks are used to write on them. The second one is a whiteboard, which has a glossy white surface; special whiteboard pens must be used to write on this board. The third type of board is the paperboard where a number of sheets of blank paper are clipped to a board or stand so that the instructor can write on them with felt-tip pens.

Before using the board, plan the work; this is the board plan. The board plan is a sketch of the planned board work on a piece of paper. The board plan should consider the following points:

- The size of the board
- How to divide the board effectively?
- The amount of information you want to put on the board.

The board plan will ensure that the information will fit on the board and that it will be presented in logical and understandable manner.

While writing on the board, take care of the following DOs and DON'Ts.

DOs

- Write legibly.
  Printing is the best; usual size of letters, which can be read without problems, is two inches.
- Write quickly.
  Use abbreviations that trainees will recognize, and only put key words.
- Allow trainees to copy down writing.
  Write on the board. Walk to one side. When you can see that everyone has stopped writing, start to explain your point.
- Use signposts.
  Numbers, letters or dashes are good signposts that will reinforce the relative importance of the points.
- Use colours to differentiate sections and points.
  Colour helps you to break the visual monotony; but do not over/do it.
- Periodically walk back to the room and check your board work for visibility, clarity, layout and colour.

DON'Ts

- Don't talk to the board.
- Don't stand in front of the board after you have written on it.
- Don't use invisible colours.

Some advanced techniques used in board work are discussed in what follows.

(a) Magnetic Displays

This requires a board with a metal base. With such a board buy plastic strips impregnated with magnetic powder available in most training equipment supply stores. One side of the strips can be used for writing with the other side stuck to the board, or the strips can be attached to cardboard with writing for the opposite side. The advantage of this magnetic display is that instead of wasting time in writing or drawing on the board during the lectures, it is possible to stick the signs as you talk. Another advantage is that pictures and signs frequently used can be kept in the hand and used whenever necessary.

(b) Prepared Charts

This is a large piece of paper on which you visually present some information or important points. Several charts, when hung from a stand, can be flipped over as each point is introduced. The advantage of this technique is that you can use charts repeatedly and save lot of time during the lecture hours. They provide an effective display of selected information.

10.3.2 Overhead Projector

They are used to project images or writing from a transparency onto a big white screen. Figure 10.1 shows a diagram of a projector.

Overhead projectors have the following advantages:

1. Have very high visual impact.
2. Save session time.
3. Give a high degree of control over what trainees will see and when they can see it.
4. Allow high degree of freedom for the trainer's imagination. ·

There are basically two types of transparencies. The first is the write-on transparency, which is a clear acetate sheet used with special coloured pens to write or draw anything. The second is the photocopy transparency. To make images on the transparencies simply pass the specially treated acetate sheet through a plain photocopier or a laser printer, both of which work on the same technology. This transparency has the advantage of being able to use the reduction and enlargement capabilities of photocopiers. The overhead projector is one of the main training tools and is commonly used in various training programs. Covering all the information is beyond the scope of this book, so, a few important points for the efficient use of the overhead projector are highlighted.

• Attach each transparency to a cardboard frame (or mount). This makes the transparency easier to handle and prevents buckling due to the heat from the glass stage and folding during storage.

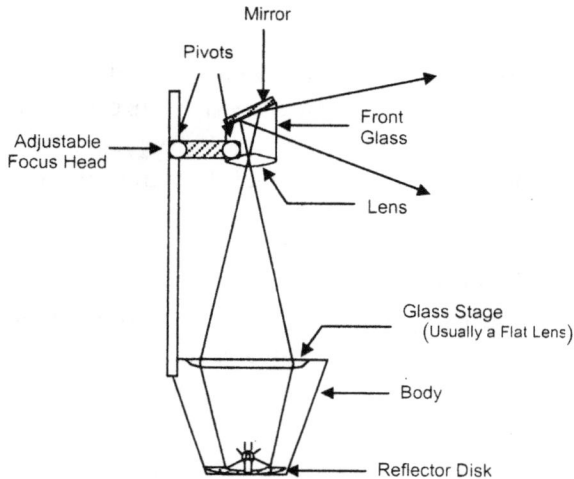

Fig. 10.1 Diagram of a Projector

- When pointing to a particular word or item, lay a pencil or similar pointer on the transparency. This will create shadow pointing to the word. Do not try to hold the pointer as you may not hold it steadily.
- Use a piece of paper between the transparency and the glass stage to mask areas and progressively uncover them to emphasize particular points.

10.3.3 Audiovisual Training Aids

Even though audiovisual training aids are expensive, they have several advantages over board works and overhead projectors. There are four main types of audiovisual units.

- Slides
- Audiotapes
- Motion picture
- Video

Let us have a brief description of these.

- **Slides**

  There are various sizes of slides available in the market but the most common is 35 mm. Slides are better at presenting "real" scenes. They are also better in illustrating images taken through a microscope or technical illustrations.

- **Audiotapes**

  Audiotapes in cassette forms are easy to handle and can have significant impact if used to provide demonstrations of sounds that a trainee may need to know about. In medical schools these are used to convey heart sounds in different disease conditions. This allows the students to hear rare and frequent sounds without disturbing the patients. Audiotapes can be used in similar training situations.

- **Motion Pictures**

  Several formats of motion picture technology are used for training and demonstration in industry and services. The major advantages of this type of audiovisual technology are its life-like representation (using colour, motion, and integrated sound) and its suitability for presenting to large audiences.

- **Video**

  They have the same advantage as motion pictures, including suitability for relatively large audiences if used with large screens (screens of 5 ft. or more are available). There is the additional advantage in that it is possible to custom-make a video. Videos can be used to demonstrate rare procedures or incidents. A real time recorded videotape of the resuscitation of a cardiac arrest or a rescue mission in a fire may give valuable information to trainees.

10.3.4 Models

In addition to the above training tools, models also can be used in training programs whenever necessary. A model could be used in the following situations:

- When the objects cannot be visualized by normal eye or with the help of microscopes (atoms, DNA, viruses).
- When accessing the real thing is not feasible for practical reasons (human models for cardio pulmonary resuscitation training).
- When the actual parts are very expensive. (In some high-tech areas.)

10.4 TRAINING FOR DIFFERENT PERSONNEL[2]

With the above ideas about the importance, psychology and tools of training, it is now possible to develop a training program for different personnel in a company. Teaching everyone everything may sound like an attractive suggestion but it is not a practical possibility; not only will it cost a lot of money, the program will not be interesting or relevant to most employees who will easily forget what they have learnt. For training purposes, it is important to divide the personnel within a company into different groups. They can be divided into the following groups:

- Investors and Upper Management.
- Middle Managers, Professionals, Technicians and Supervisors.

- Quality Control Inspectors and Quality Checkers
- Regular Workers

It is efficient to divide up the groups in this way as each of them has a different responsibility for TQM implementation. Let us see how the training program for each group can be organized for the best results.

10.4.1 Training for Investors and Upper Management

The basic motive of investors and upper management is to make profit. This is natural in a free market economy. Even though quality management concepts do not work against profit, too great an emphasis on profit or trying to make short cuts for short-term profits will result in poor quality. A training program for investors should emphasize how TQM implementation will produce long-term results although there will be some short-term sacrifices. There should be an emphasis on the following areas: commitment to continuous improvement, customer satisfaction and the importance of training.

Most quality management consultants are of the opinion that training for investors and upper management should take place outside their investment places, so they will concentrate on the message. Their attention can be attracted with detailed case studies of companies that have gone into bankruptcy because of poor qualities and stories of the successful implementation of TQM. Providing information about the problems faced by middle managers in implementing TQM will also help ensure that middle managers get the necessary cooperation later on. A quality management consultant usually conducts the training for this level.

10.4.2 Training for Middle Managers, Professionals, Technicians and Supervisors

The most difficult tasks in implementing TQM program lies with these people. They have to balance the profit requirements of upper management while ensuring that TQM programs are implemented without setbacks. The main responsibility of identifying the root causes and overcoming them lies with this group. Training programs for these people need to be detailed and contain most of the main concepts such as: understanding the production process, the importance of customer satisfaction, the importance of measurement, root cause identification, the importance of communication, motivating employees, the importance of training people and the challenges of implementation.

Training should take place in a location close to the production area where this important group of personnel can develop an idea of how to implement TQM principles in practice. It should include detailed lectures with visual aids as well as group discussions and on-site demonstrations for better performance. Quality circles are the tools that will bring about coordination and cultural exchange between these people. Either the quality management consultant or one of the consultant's team members conducts training programs for these people.

10.4.3 Training for Quality Inspectors and Quality Checkers

Quality checkers and quality inspectors perform one of the important functions of TQM implementation: identifying non-conforming materials and entering information about these materials in appropriate places. So when selecting and training people for quality checking functions, care must be taken to choose people who will pay attention to detail and be able to identify mistakes and record information about such mistakes in the appropriate place without bias. The training program for such people must give emphasis to the importance of accurate measurement and root cause identification.

This group of personnel should be trained in a location near the work site or actually in the work site. The quality control manager or other professionals will usually conduct the training. The training programs can use the necessary visual aids and models to explain what is being tested and how.

10.4.4 Training for Workers

Workers are central to the quality revolution; nothing can be achieved without their cooperation. Providing information and some education about the changes that are planned will engage the cooperation of the workers. Training programs should provide an understanding of the production process, the importance of customer satisfaction and communication as well as the problems that might be encountered during implementation. Training should also provide a brief idea of quality management tools that will help inspire confidence in them.

The most convenient training site would be the work site, or somewhere close to the work site. Training should be conducted by the supervisor; this will not only be convenient but will also develop better communication between the workers and the management. Training could include visual aids such as videotapes, prepared with the help of actors, to explain the importance of ideas such as customer satisfaction in an interesting and understandable way.

10.5 TRAINING FOR THE SERVICE SECTOR

All the factors that have been discussed so far are useful and relevant when discussing training in the service sector. One important difference between the production and service sector is that in the service sector, most of the bottom-line employees come into direct contact with customers. Training programs for bottom-line workers should emphasize customer satisfaction so that employees can understand how to tackle customer behavior in a wide variety of situations.

Chapter Eleven

IMPLEMENTING QUALITY IMPROVEMENT

11.1 CHALLENGES OF IMPLEMENTATION

It is often the case that a company or organization that would like to make change is ready and prepared to make change but finally nothing happens. This also happens with individuals, for example many students intend to prepare conscientiously for exams but finally escape before the exam with a medical excuse.

There are a number of reasons for this problem: poor commitment, poor planning, poor implementation and, in some instances, personality problems and so on. The key thing to understand is that nothing will happen unless someone does something. In quality management 'doing something' is changing the culture and management style of the company.

Changing the culture is not an easy objective to achieve. Section 3.4 discussed the idea that time is needed for change. This is well illustrated by Deming's words "a big ship travelling in full speed requires distance and time to turn around". When talking about cultural change a feasible timeframe could be 'generations'. One generation consists of 33 years; this does not mean that 33 years are needed to implement a quality management program in a company. Depending on the size and problems of the company, the time needed may vary from 3 to 15 years or more. But a total change of society towards quality—quality products, quality services and a quality environment in which to live—may take one or two generations after everyone has fully committed towards the goal.

Let us now discuss the components of change and the procedures for making a change.

11.2 MAKING A CHANGE

The changes that take place around us can be grouped into two major categories. The first is 'natural', that is changes that occur as a result of the natural and intrinsic quality of the things and organism. The second type is 'intended' changes that are conceived by human beings. Although natural changes are unavoidable and influence the quality of work a great deal, they are beyond the scope of this book. In the context of quality management, it is more useful to discuss intended change. When discussing change it is important to accept one central fact. Although there is a clearly identifiable need for change and many advantages will result from it, the behaviour of human groups and culture is extremely resistant to change. Despite this resistance, changes take place as a result of necessity and as a way of survival.

11.2.1 Components of a Changing Process[14]

Psychologists have identified different components in the process of change. A brief discussion of these components will help implement a smooth program of change within companies and organizations. There are seven basic components in the change process: need, awareness, experimenting, motivation, commitment, letting go and restructuring. Before analysing these processes it is necessary to mention here that they need not be sequential. They are highly integrated and different people arrange them in different orders. Let us now brief these components and see how they fit within the history of TQM.

- **Need**

   It is clear that no changes occur without a need. Quality management is a very good example of this. Even though the main quality management consultants originated in America, the Second World War created a need for them in Japan and it was a necessity that made Japanese industry accept quality management concepts. Even though American managers ignored quality management principles initially, economic depression in 1970s made them think about it. Even if there is a great deal of wonderful knowledge, it will not be accepted or implemented without a need.

- **Awareness**

   The second component of change is awareness. Awareness is consciousness of the existence of a need and the necessity of satisfying that need. It is usually expressed as an awareness of stress, distress or an unsatisfied condition of mind. An encounter with problems of poor quality, either in society or management, leads to stress and an awareness that something must be done to solve it.

- **Experimentation**

  Having developed a need and awareness for change, the change is not made immediately. As discussed previously, several factors prevent the implementation of immediate change. Often what happens is that a few individuals who are daring and forward-thinking— sometimes such people are labelled as antisocial even terrorist, e.g. Galileo— make changes at the experimental level and produce some initial gains.

  If they are successful in their attempts everyone becomes motivated to follow their example, but if they are not successful, society becomes even more resistant to change and the same routines are followed until someone tries the experiment again and shows some success.

- **Motivation**

  If the individual is successful after experimentation, then news begins to spread through society. As a result, there is a great deal of motivation towards making change. The usual motivation for social change comes from news agencies, government programs and informal groups.

- **Commitment**

  Commitment for change comes as a result of motivation. However, even if there are some success stories, culture and society may still resist the implementation of change. Only a strong commitment can help break down barriers preventing implementation; this is the major problem in TQM implementation.

- **Letting Go**
  Where there is a strong commitment, even if some barriers remain, the letting go stage will be achieved. Even though it is new and some people will not like it, most people will begin to accept what is taking place around them.

- **Restructuring**
  Restructuring is a long-run process which will change every one, every branch and every field. Even though computers were basically invented to do digital and analog calculation, they do not stop at level, they are changing everyone and everything nowadays. It is an unavoidable phase and any mismanagement can lead to big social distress and personal disruptions.

11.2.2 Breaking the Barriers

An analysis of the problems towards change within a company will show that there are many points of resistance. There is resistance not only from management but also from supervisors, the workforce and even from unions. The reasons for such resistance are many and include social factors such as a tight system of beliefs, habits and traditional practices alongside personal factors such as rigid personality and the fear of being left out. To overcome such resistance, the following techniques will be useful.

- **Providing Participation**
  All of those who will be involved in the change, and all those who might be affected by the change should be allowed to participate in the planning execution

of change. In such a team every participant should be treated with dignity and every opinion and complaint should be heard with a positive attitude. Working in this way will help to develop a favourable social climate for the changes that have to be made. Such teamwork not only prevents the feeling of being left out but also provides opportunities for the evaluation of the merits of the plan.

- **Giving Training**

  It is better to train the existing workforce to implement a new technique rather than hiring or taking new people from outside the company. This not only prevents hassles inside the company but also prevents the loss of experienced and valuable workforce. When dealing with resistance from middle management to TQM implementation, training might be the best solution. In addition to detailed training for the management in quality management techniques, introductory training in quality management tools for all bottom line employees might be more useful in removing unnecessary fear and obtaining full co-operation.

- **Providing Adequate Time**

  In all instances, adequate time should be allowed for the acceptance of change. Indeed, it takes time to evaluate and accommodate the merits and demerits of change. Frustration and impatience at the delay in implementing change never helps; such attitudes may cause the resistance to become more acute.

- **Formation of Informal Groups**
  In any cultural change, either in a company or in society as a whole, informal groups can act to break down barriers and enlist the cooperation of all. In quality management these groups are known as quality circles, but in society these groups can function under many different names. Informal groups work together on an equal basis to strengthen team spirit, help in the setting and attainment of reasonable targets, improve morale and communication, promote initiative and finally help to achieve the total cultural change that is being expected.

An in-depth knowledge of change will help in the effective management of a process of change and will also help solve problems that may be encountered during the process. With this basic idea, let us now discuss other issues related to implementation.

11.3   DIVISION OF RESPONSIBILITY AMONGST PERSONNEL[2]

In TQM implementation different personnel working in the organization will hold different responsibilities. A clear understanding of the different responsibilities and the relationships between them will help implement the quality management program without confusion. The relationships between the different personnel working inside an organization can be explained as in Figure 11.1.

Even though Figure 11.1 can provide an understanding of the relationships between different personnel inside a company, it is not necessary that the number of employees need to be the same as in the figure. For example in a department with 25-30 people, the quality control manager, middle manager and professional could be a single individual. But in such instances we should make sure that all the responsibilities of three different personnel are completed by such a person without any delay.

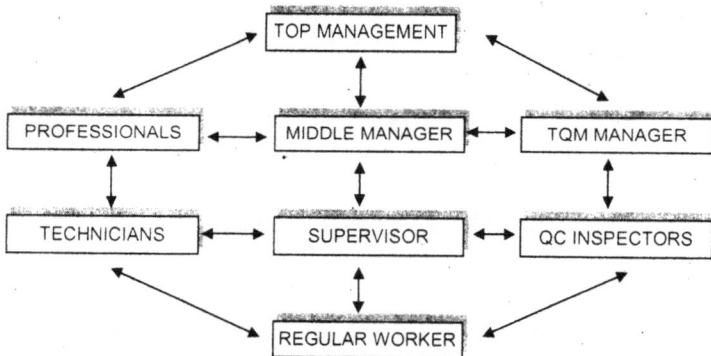

Fig. 11.1 Relationships between Personnel Inside the Company

Let us now discuss the different responsibilities of the different groups of personnel within the company.

(a) **Top Management and Investors**

- Make a strong commitment towards quality and be prepared to sacrifice some short-term profit.
- Be in continuous communication with and be physically available to the middle managers to assure them of personal determination on this subject.
- Ensure that necessary funding is allocated to the training and other quality management programs.
- Ensure that a well-organized motivation system is in action in the company.

- Ensure that a complete suggestion system is functioning in the company and that all of the intelligence and talent of all employees are being directed towards the growth of the company.

(b) Middle Managers and Supervisors

- Ensure that quality requirements for their worksite are identified and met on time.
- Facilitate communication between different personnel.
- Take responsibility for training and other quality management programs.
- Work with employees to identify their talents and personal needs so that every employee gets adequate motivation.

(c) Professionals and Technicians

- Take responsibility for identifying the requirements and help others to achieve these requirements.
- Help in identifying root causes and solving technical problems.
- Help in training of technical skills.
- Communicate with employees to identify improvement ideas.

(d) Quality Control Managers and Inspectors

- Take responsibility for ensuring that outgoing products are according to conformance requirements.
- Record information about non-conforming materials accurately into non-conformance material databases.

- Take responsibility for analysing information about non-conforming material and discovering root causes.
- Training employees for and maintaining a quality checking system.

(e) Regular Workers

- Ensure that procedures are followed.
- Report any confusion over procedures or quality of the products to the management.
- Help identify improved techniques in production line.
- Report any problems regarding working conditions to the management.

11.4 IMPLEMENTING CORRECTIVE ACTION[8]

All of the issues previously discussed, from identifying customer expectations to training, are important for the smooth implementation of corrective action; but the implementation process will not be smooth and trouble-free even if everything else is done perfectly. There is still a lot of discussion on the best way of doing things. Quality management consultants disagree on what to do when non-conforming material is received; either stop the entire process or allow it to run with similar other issues. Before going further into these issues, we will now discuss the different steps that have to be followed in an implementation program.

11.4.1 Steps in an Implementation Program

Generally we can divide an effective implementation program into seven steps as listed below.

- Defining the situation
- Identifying and applying the fix
- Identifying the root causes
- Generation of possible corrective actions
- Selection of the best corrective action
- Implementation of corrective action
- Evaluation and holding of gains

Let us discuss each step in more detail.

Defining the Situation

Before attempting to solve a problem, it is important to define it in simple terms; while defining it the following points have to be considered.

- Use simple words.
- Use definite terms whenever possible.
  Size of the problem (in terms of PONC),
  Location of the problem.
- Do not give an opinion or try to blame anyone.
- Give the duration of the problem.
  (This is considered very important in medical field.)

Identifying and Applying a Fix

After defining the problem and before planning the corrective action, a fix has to be applied. A fix is a temporary and symptomatic treatment that will not solve the causes of the problem. It basically patches up the process until a permanent solution is in place. Examples of fixes include:

- Reworking or repairing non-conforming output.
- Replacing a sub-product from outside the company.
- Emergency measures in case of outbreak of a disease.

A fix will give immediate relief and time to think about the problem; it may also have dangerous consequences, as there is a tendency to continue with the fix instead of solving the problem forever. Such habits can even lead to the destruction of the company as a whole.

Identifying Root Causes

After applying the fix there will be time to analyse the problem and to identify the causes of problems. All the issues from the chapters on "Measurement" and "root causes" will have to be considered. The final result will be several charts and tables that will help track the basic causes of the problem. These tools alongside a suggestion system that will help mobilize the intelligence of employees will help discover the root cause of the problem.

Generation of Possible Corrective Actions

The next step after discovering the root cause is to identify as many corrective actions as possible to solve the problem. A brain storming session may be of great value. Experiences from the past, and experience of other companies can also give some hints. The next step is the documentation of the possible action plan.

Selecting the Best Corrective Action

The corrective actions have to be evaluated against factors such as cost, time for implementation, complexity of implementation and so on. Whenever possible there should be a small-scale experimental evaluation of each technique.

One of the most important factors that need consideration in the selection of the best corrective action is 'mistake-proofing'. Mistake-proofing makes it impossible for non-conformance to be unknowingly passed on to the customer. An example of mistake-proofing is a computer program that will not allow further inputs if there is an error. A corrective action that mistake proofs the process ensures that non-conformance is permanently eliminated. It must also be remembered that when defects are produced as a result of poor knowledge in the techniques of production, trying to implement a mistake proofing system will not only produce stress among employees but also can hold up production permanently.

Implementing Corrective Action

After selecting the best corrective action, the next step will be implementing the corrective action. Implementation will constitute three components: communication, training and making the necessary changes. Communication about corrective action should be done through formal and informal groups that will help identify and solve any problem during implementation and also ensure the cooperation of everyone involved. The problems regarding communication were discussed in Chapter Nine.

The next component in implementing corrective action will be training. As explained in the Chapter on "training", all employees should be trained in the new techniques and quality management concepts. The third component in implementing corrective action will be making the necessary changes. This includes changing procedures, changing documents, changing equipment and managing the psychological components of change effectively.

Evaluation and Holding the Gains [Doing Everything Once Again]

Having implemented change, the next step in the program is evaluating and holding the gains. One of the most important concepts in continuous quality improvement is doing everything once again. Once you have achieved something you have to evaluate your achievements and take the necessary action to hold these gains. This includes appreciating the work done, making the necessary document changes and restructuring the work and training programs. An important fact that has to be accepted is that when one problem has been solved, the next problem is waiting. In production and service problems occur for many reasons. Once a problem has been solved this does not mean that it will not arise again. This requires constant activity in identifying and solving problems. The term *continuous quality improvement* came as a result of this concept. Without such an attitude, the gains cannot be held. Problems occur in everyday life and solving them is an art and part of human living. Only a person who knows this art and is capable of solving problems can be a successful person.

11.4.2 A Practical Situation

A practical situation might help understand all of the steps and concepts behind implementation. Imagine a factory with 3000 employees and 15 departments that is producing motorbikes. The company does not have a specific quality management programme and the level of non-conformance at the finishing line varies from 10–20 percent. A mass inspection at the end of the production line ensures that 98 percent of products are defect-free when going out into the market. The identified defective goods are either sent for rework or discarded as scrap. Even though prices are a little high, the company is in a controlled economy without competition and so there are enough sales to make a profit.

However, the government suddenly decides to open up the market for international competition. As a result, cheaper and better quality motorbikes start to arrive in the market. This situation imposes a big pressure on the company to increase quality and decrease price.

Usually companies in such situations try to improve quality by spending more money on mass inspections. Certainly this will help increase quality, but the price will increase as well. So how should the company increase the quality and decrease the price? Suppose you are hired as the quality management consultant, what would you do to improve the quality?

The first thing is to check the commitment of upper management towards quality. Are they really serious in making quality products and services or do they work on short-term profit motive? It is also important to find out whether management is really ready to spend the initial expenditure needed for the quality improvement program. All quality consultants agree that without a strong commitment from upper management nothing can be achieved in quality. If upper management does not have a strong commitment, the techniques outlined in this book can be tried, but if they still do not understand the problem then it is better to stay away as the company can become the next 'Titanic' at any time.

Having decided to implement a TQM system inside the company, trying to go to every department and identifying non-conformance areas and then correcting them will disturb everybody and every process and lead to a big mess. What is the best thing to do?

First, identify a department with poor quality and attempt to help them improve their quality. As discussed earlier, try to identify some fix that may relieve the problem for a short while. This may be the introduction of a checking device in the production line to remove scrap or finding a replacement for a sub-product from outside the company. While doing so, ensure that employees do not accept the fix as a permanent solution; this will perpetuate the problem forever.

Really solving the problem of that department means starting the journey from customer satisfaction to implementation, following the steps outlined from Chapter Three to Chapter Eleven.

The process will vary from place to place and situation to situation; it is not possible to cover all the different situations here. The only people who can help, above and beyond your own intelligence, education and experience are senior bottom-line workers and technicians who are often waiting for a chance to communicate their, wonderful, solutions to the problems they encounter on a day-to-day basis. Establishing better communications with them, mobilizing their intelligence through an organized suggestion system will provide all the necessary technical information for improving the quality of output from a given work area.

If everything is fine and moves smoothly then an improvement in quality may be seen in around three months. While making the changes permanent and holding gains, the process should be expanded to other areas. Looking at departments individually and training the people who work within them can inspire the quality revolution. Everyone should be allowed to participate in the planning and implementation of the process while employees should be given enough time to accept change and so avoid any stress or fear in the change process.

11.4.3 Which is the Best Technique

As we have seen earlier, there is a lot of discussion on the relative merits of different quality management techniques: mass inspection or SPC; zero defect or AQL; stopping the process or allowing it to run when non-conformance is reported. Now we will discuss about these problems briefly.

Mass Inspection or SPC

All management consultants agree that mass inspection is an old way of implementing quality checking and should be substituted by SPC, which means checking intermediate products and other environmental factors to prevent quality problems in the final products. Implementing SPC does not necessarily mean that the final product does not have to be checked for quality problems. Whenever necessary, arrangements have to be made to check the final product for defects but SPC prevents stress in such final checking by giving better quality products for checking and also saves a lot of money by identifying defects at earlier levels and thereby preventing scraps at the final stage.

Another practice introduced in SPC is sampling QC. It is time and money-saving and appropriate in many instances. But again it is not necessary to be strict about it. Wherever it is possible to perform QC by affordable automated electronic devices, 100 per cent quality checking can be instituted. It is also best to implement 100 per cent quality checking whenever defect-free products or services (e.g. medical services) are expected. or if defects in any product can cause a greater magnitude of problems in the next production line.

On-line Inspection or Off-line Inspection

On-line inspection means quality checking all products and allowing products to pass only after they are checked for defects while off-line inspection involves sampling QC on selected products without disturbing the production process. Which is the best technique? It depends on the situation. We can list situations for each technique as follows:

1. On-line Inspection

- Whenever there are quality problems reported frequently.
- When allowing defects will produce a greater magnitude of problem and waste in the next step.
- Whenever 100 per cent defect free products and services are expected.

2. Off-line Inspection

- When there are reports of good quality in products.

- When it is known that products will be checked again and defects do not cause major problems in the next step.
- When defective products can be allowed into market as replacing them does not cost much.

The above guidelines can help in deciding whether to implement on-line or off-line inspection.

Zero Defect or AQL

Philip B. Crosby introduced the 'zero-defect' philosophy to emphasize the importance of preventing any single defect being released into the market and explained how AQL can cause major problems in quality and customer satisfaction. Even though zero defect is a good philosophy to follow, it has some weaknesses. Deciding to implement sampling QC means accepting, AQL as well so that once this policy has been accepted it is technically not possible to produce Zero Defect; next one trying to implement it where defects are due to poor knowledge can cause stress and dissatisfaction within employees.

Stop the Process or Allow it to Run

Quality management consultants have discussed whether it is better to stop a production line completely or allow it to run once non-conformance has been reported. The following have to be considered before making a decision. As discussed in Chapter Seven, any variable line will not be straight or flat. There will be small fluctuations with occasional spikes. The reasons for these problems have already been discussed. If the reason is known and can be corrected, stopping the whole process is unnecessary. In addition, accidents may happen without anyone to be blamed. If a mistake has happened accidentally, disturbing all employees and the entire process is unnecessary.

Another reason for allowing the process to run is to discover the cause of the problem. In some instances trying to stop the process when non-conformance is reported and then finding the cause of the problem is impossible. In such instances allowing the process to run at a low level is important in trying to trace the root cause of the problem.

While all these reasons justify running the process, it should be stopped once the cause of the problem is known, and only by stopping can the root cause be corrected and quality improved.

Just in Time or Buffer Stock

Another subject that is being discussed by quality management consultants is whether to follow the 'just in time' procedure or to maintain a buffer stock of raw materials, sub-products and products. Chapter Two gives an explanation of what is meant by 'just in time'. Briefly, it means that production will only be done when there is an order from the next production section. The 'just in time' procedure tries to prevent the blockage of capital in the form of stock and storage space. Even though the 'just in time' system has several advantages, it has its disadvantages as well. Stopping and starting production according to orders means that the workforce will have to alternate between working hard and sitting down. This will not only make manpower expensive but will also create a lot of disturbance amongst the employees.

The solution is to maintain a buffer stock within two limits: a minimum limit at which orders have to be produced and a maximum limit at which either purchases or production has to be stopped. In this way, it is possible to produce a constant working environment and a good supply of resources for production.

11.5 IMPLEMENTING IN THE SERVICE SECTOR

As discussed earlier in Chapter One, the service sector, especially the social services such as health education and government, are tightly regulated by strict rules and regulations. Therefore, making changes according to the expectations and experiences of employees is not always possible. But this does not necessarily mean that nothing can be done from experience. What is needed is a widespread suggestion system. Instead of a suggestion system inside the company, as in industry, we have to create and maintain a well-organized suggestion system that links employees to professionals and lawmakers. For example a schoolteacher should be linked to the professor of education and the minister of education. Such suggestion systems are made possible today by the Internet and intranet technologies. A system such as this will make it possible to carry out studies from time to time and implement actions to improve quality.

In addition, even though we do not have the right to change the content of the service provided it is possible to change the way in which the service is provided. For example, measures such as modifying the timetable to suit the convenience of the pupils will bring better cooperation from the service users.

This concludes the discussion of quality management concepts. All the discussion is aimed at giving a clear understanding of quality management concepts. For further discussion and explanation, consult one of the reference books that are listed in the references.

Chapter Twelve

SCIENTIFIC METHOD OF PROBLEM SOLVING

12.1 INTRODUCTION TO SCIENTIFIC METHODS

If you read a book written by a quality management consultant you will certainly come across the importance of science and scientific methods of problem-solving in quality management practice. Science is certainly one of the important factors which help human civilization achieve success. Even though the main scientific inventions started to come around the 18th century, the roots of scientific thinking can be tracked as far back as Greek and Roman civilizations. What is science or what is the definition of science? Even though science helps us solve problems and define the knowledge, finding a single definitions for science is not possible. There are simple definitions like "method of solving problems" and complicated definitions like "systematic approach to extension of existing knowledge and common sense".

Even though each definition is justifiable in different circumstances, it is better to consider science as a method of solving problems for the TQM discussion because it not only is simple but also gives direct relation to TQM, which tries to solve problems in the production and service sector. In a scientific method how are problems solved? Basically, problems are approached in five different steps to find a solution.

Step 1: Identifying Problems
Here problems are identified and defined. When doing so, you have to divide the problem as small as possible and try to define each problem in simple definite terms easy to understand.

Step 2: Formulating Alternative Explanations
After identifying problems, alternate explanations or solutions are formulated. Each of them will explain or give a solution to the problems in a different way, in a different angle or in a different philosophy.

Step 3: Conducting Experiments
Here each alternative is tested for accuracy. What has been done here is small-scale experimental activity for each alternative under different control condition and the results are recorded.

Step 4: Analyzing Results
The results of experiments are analyzed to find out the best explanation or solution for the problem.

Step 5: Finding the Solution
According to analysis, the best explanation or solution is identified and implemented.

One important point we have to keep in mind is that we are selecting only the best alternative; it does not necessarily need to be the correct alternative. This concept is explained as "Science accepts lies as truth until truth gets identified". In practical content it is important for us, as when we reached one solution for a problem it is not the end of the subject. Till the absolute answer gets identified, we have more room for experiments and analysis.

12.2 SCIENTIFIC METHOD IN SOCIAL SCIENCES[15]

The above-explained method is acceptable for fields like physics or chemistry, even to some extent in biology. But when coming to fields like psychology or sociology, it is not possible to conduct experiments as we wish. For example, if you want to identify the effects of smoking in different age groups you can't select people from different age groups and ask them to smoke for a period and conduct the testing. For social ethics, such experiments won't be allowed in our society. What we usually do here is there are already people smoking in the society. Select them and try to conduct your study on them. This technique is usually explained as 'research method'. Let us have a brief description of the components of the social research.

Basically, seven different components can be identified in a social research execution. They are:

1. Defining research problems,
2. Reviewing the literature,
3. Formulating the hypothesis,
4. Researching design,
5. Collecting the data,
6. Analyzing the data,
7. Interpreting and reporting.

While a small and simple research can be done by executing the above steps in order from 1 to 7,

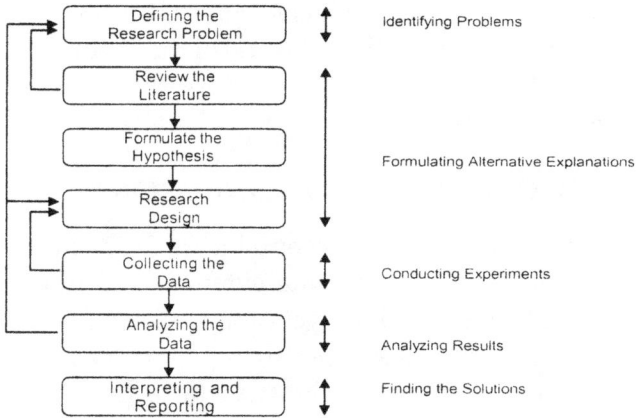

Fig. 12.1 Components of Research Methodology

complicated big researches will have several feedbacks and take quite a long time before completion. Figure 12.1 may give you the possible sequential order of execution of these components and identical components of scientific methods from Section 12.1.

Now let us describe each component briefly.

1. Defining Research Problem

As we explained earlier, here, we have to define our problem in clear and definite terms. This task of formulating or defining a research problem is a step of greatest importance in the entire research process. Professor W.A. Neiswanger correctly states that the statement of the objective is of basic importance because it determines the data which are to be collected, the characteristics of the data which are relevant, relations which are to be exposed, the choice of techniques to be used in these explorations and the form of the final report.

2. Reviewing the Literature

Once the problem is formulated, a brief summary of it should be written down. For this, the researcher should undertake extensive literature survey connected with the problem. The following activities are done for this purpose. Journals and surveys published and unpublished bibliographies and abstracted and indexed. The earlier studies, if any, which are similar to the present study, should be carefully studied. A good library will be a great help to the researcher at this stage.

3. Formulating Hypotheses

After extensive literature survey, the researcher should state in clear terms the hypothesis or working hypothesis. It is a tentative assumption made in order to draw out its logical and empirical consequences. They are very important as they provide the focal point for the research. They also affect the manner in which tests must be conducted in the analysis of the data and, indirectly, the quality of data, which is required for the analysis. Hypothesis should be very specific and limited to the piece of research in hand because it has to be tested. The role of hypothesis is to guide the researcher by delimiting the area of research and keep him on the right track. It sharpens the thinking and focuses attention on the more important factors of the problem. It also indicates the type of data required and the type of methods for data analysis to be used.

4. Designing the Research

After the research problem has been formulated in clear-cut terms, the researcher will be required to prepare a

research design, a conceptual structure within which
research would be conducted. The preparation of such
research design is to provide for the collection of relevant
evidence with minimal expenditure of effect, time and
money.

The preparation of the research design, appropriate
for a particular research problem, usually involves the
consideration of the following:

i.   The means of obtaining the information.
ii. The availability and skills of the researcher and
     his staff (if any).
iii. Explanation of the way in which selected means
     of obtaining information will be organized and
     the reasoning leading to the selection.
iv. The time available for research.
v.   The cost factor relating to research, i.e. the finance
     available for the purpose.

Deciding about appropriate sampling technique is
also a part of the research design. Sampling technique
will be discussed in more detail in Chapter Thirteen.
Now let us see what we mean by the word *sampling*.
All the items under consideration in any field of inquiry
constitute a 'universe' or 'population'. A complete
enumeration of all the items in the population is known
as *census inquiry*. It is usually presumed that in such an
inquiry the highest accuracy of information can be
obtained. But in practice this may not be true. Even a
slight element of bias in any means in such an inquiry
will get larger and larger as the number of observation
increases. In addition this type of inquiry involves a
greater deal of time, money and energy. Not only this,
census inquiry is not possible in practice under many

circumstances. For instance, blood testing is done only on sample basis. Hence, quite often we select only a few items from the universe for our study purpose. The form so selected constitutes what is technically called a sample. In research design the researcher must decide the way of selecting a sample or what is popularly known as the *sample design*.

5. Collecting the Data (Execution of Research)

There are different techniques used to collect data. The most appropriate technique will depend on the type of study; information needed to be collected with other factors like context of money costs, time and other recourses at the disposal of the researcher. Let us see some data collecting techniques.

(a) Observation

This method implies the collection of information by way of investigator's own observation, without interviewing the respondents. The information obtained relates to what is currently happening and is not complicated by either the past behaviour or future intentions or attitudes of the respondents. This technique is used to identify the behaviour of individuals or groups in different circumstances.

(b) Interviews

The investigator follows a rigid procedure and seeks answers to a set of pre-conceived questions through personal interviews. This method of collecting data is usually carried out in a structured way where output depends upon the ability of the interviewer to a large extent. Such interviews can be carried out by different techniques:

- Through personal interviews
- Through telephone interviews
- By mailing of questionnaires
- Through enumerators and trained interviewers

In all these methods questionnaires are used to collect information. It is better to examine the efficiency of the questionnaire through a pilot study before starting the actual research.

(c) Warranty Cards

Warranty cards are used by service providers and marketing institutions to collect information about customers for their business purposes during social researches. These cards are delivered to customers inside the package along with the products with a request to the consumer to fill it and post it back to the dealer. Probably it could be the best way to collect information about the likes and dislikes, but such questionnaires should not be too long; if they are, poor compliance and biased information will result.

(d) Depth Interviews

Depth interviews are those interviews that are designed to discover underlying motives and desires and are often used in motivational research, such interviews are held to explore needs, desires and feelings of respondents. In other words, they aim to elicit unconscious components of personality as also other types of material relating, especially to personality dynamics and motivations. As such, depth interviews require great skill on the part of the interviewer and involve considerable time. Unless the researcher has specialized training, depth interview should not be attempted.

(e) Content Analyses

Content analysis consists of analyzing the content of documentary materials such as books, magazines, newspapers and content of all other verbal materials, which can be either spoken or printed. The analysis of content is a central activity whenever one is concerned with the study of the nature of the verbal materials. Such study can help to get valuable information about market situations. Content analysis can be done on secondary sources of data like personal letters, logs and other government periodicals like census, health statistics, statistical records, government reports, mass communication materials and government commission reports.

(f) Projective Techniques

It is an indirect method to study people's attitudes and emotions. Projective techniques have the capacity to bring out the deeper personality of the respondent without his awareness. A stimulus is given to the respondent and the respondent is freely allowed to express his opinions. As they mostly deal with personality structure, they are normally used in clinical research and practice.

(g) Case Study Method

The case study method is a careful and a complete observation of a social unit. Such unit can be a person, a family, an institution, a cultural group or even the entire community. It is a method of study in depth rather than breadth. For example you can conduct a case study of a company that recently went bankrupt or a company that made success in the market. In sociology and psychology, case study methods are used to get information from rare events. Example: case study of a child who grew up with wolves and case study of a sport player who lost his profession due to drug addiction. Even though all the scientific principles are not followed in case study methods, it is very useful and the only available way to expand the knowledge in many instances.

6. Analyzing the Data

After data have been colleted, the researcher turns to the task of analyzing them. The analysis of data requires a number of closely related operations such as establishment of categories, the application of these categories to the raw data through coding, tabulation and using other statistical techniques. During the analysis we do computation of various averages, percentages, coefficients, etc. by applying various well-defined formulas.

7. Interpreting and Reporting

In this state, the test of hypothesis is done with the help of statistical techniques like Chi-square test, T-test, F-test and so on. When the researcher does not have a hypothesis to test, generalization is established on the basis of data and stated as hypothesis to be tested by successive researchers in time to come. Finally, the researcher has to prepare the report of what has been done by him. Writing the report must be done with great care keeping in view the following:

   I. The layout of the report should be as follows.
- The preliminary pages
- The starting pages
- The end matter

  II. The report should be written in a concise and objective style in simple language avoiding vague expressions.

 III. Charts and illustrations in the main report should be used only if they present the information more clearly and forcibly.

 IV. Calculated 'confidence limits' must be mentioned and the various constraints experienced in conducting the research operations be stated.

The above explanation about research methodology will help you to understand any events in conducting a research process. If you want to conduct a business research yourself then you should develop a better idea about this subject by referring to a reference book or a standard textbook in research methodology.

12.3 CLASSIFICATION OF KNOWLEDGE FIELDS[16]

So far we have seen how science helps us to solve our problems and expand our knowledge. What happens to the knowledge after expansion? Is it organized in an easy, understandable and accessible form? How to get the knowledge we want or how to find out what a particular knowledge is about. Usually a knowledge field, which developed through scientific method, ends with 'logy'—psychology, biology and so on. If you try to list all the 'logies' available today it may go above a thousand. If you go to a library and try to find out availability of books on each field of knowledge, there may be hundreds of books. In addition, today we have Internet. If you type a word in a search engine to find knowledge it may give thousands of web sites.

But we should have a basic idea how the scientific knowledge is organized [such terminology can be used for knowledge acquired by scientific methods]. Auguste Comte (1798-1857), the person considered as father of sociology, tried to arrange the knowledge fields as in Figure 12.2. It is known as Comet's Hierarchy of Sciences.

Here he considers mathematics as the fundamental of all existing knowledge we are having and arrange other fields in increasing complexity. It is a very basic

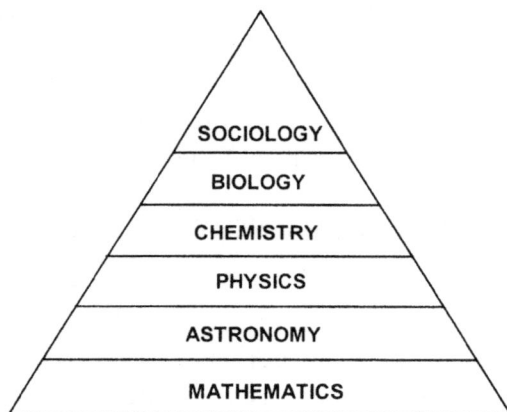

Fig. 12.2 Comet's Hierarchy of Sciences

classification of knowledge we are having and may help you to get a picture of knowledge world.

12.4 INFORMATION REVOLUTION AND CHANGING MARKET SITUATION

Today the world and market mechanism are going on a revolutionary change due to changes in the information management system. The computers and the Internet are changing our lives. World economy shows very good growth rates. Economists predict this favourable condition may last as long as 25 years. What is all this about and what is actually happening around us? How will it affect customer-producer relations and how can we understand these changes in TQM context. Let us try to understand this.

If we want to analyze the above changes, first we should understand what we mean by the word *market*. The basic definition is "meeting place of a buyer and seller where they go for a deal". It can be a physical location, it can be on the telephone line, it can be on a newspaper or it can be on the Internet. Each of these market mechanisms has its own advantages and disadvantages. Let us see what is the superiority of the market on the Internet. Basically, it brings you too many choices. By sitting in your home you can look at the choices available and select the best one. To analyze the advantages of the market on the Internet more clearly, let us try to understand how it tries to bring customer satisfaction.

Earlier we have catagorized the expectations of the customer as four As. Let us see how these As get satisfied through the Internet market system.

- The first A is Accountability. Of course it is difficult for you to determine the accountability of a product through the Internet, but this problem is usually overcome by return policy. Say if you don't like the product you can return it within a certain time period without losing any money.
- The second A is Accessibility. Certainly Internet can give you a big price list where you can select the price you like. Even though you don't have the choice to check the price in the corner store, you can rely on the Internet as more and more competitors are coming on the Internet.
- The third A is Availability. The Internet market has advantage and disadvantage on this content. In Internet market you can have a look on the goods available in any corner of the world. When you order for the goods you have to wait for the shipment to be received at you doorstep. But as several courier services are available today, such delay becomes shorter and shorter.
- The fourth A is Appearance. Internet can give you as many possible appearances as available. Even one step above can order a new appearance whenever possible.

The above explanation gives you an understanding of how the Internet can influence the market situation. It is true that every corner of the world, every home is not yet connected to the Internet. But the Internet services are expanding rapidly and over the next 10 or 20 years it is going to be the main market mechanism. While it is good news for a producer for respecting quality and using the Internet services to sell his goods, it is bad news for a person who tries to cheat his customers and sit in a corner to sell his products.

Chapter Thirteen

STATISTICS FOR MANAGERS[13]

13.1 INTRODUCTION TO STATISTICS

Statistics is a method or field of study which helps us to classify, analyze and test the accuracy of data collected through different methods. What do we mean by data? Data consist of discrete observations of attributes or events that carry a definite value but little meaning. Information is obtained by summarizing; adjusting for variation and presenting data in a logical form that could give us some understanding about the incident or problem. Information will have a definite value in contrast to opinion, which won't have a definite value. Simply this difference can be explained with the following example—'6 feet 2 inches' is a data; 'Raja is 6 feet 2 inches tall' is information, and 'Raja is taller' is an opinion.

13.2 PRESENTATION OF DATA

Data, once collected, must be arranged in an order to understand the incidents clearly and meaningfully. In statistics, we have several methods of presenting the data: tables, charts, diagrams, graphs, pictures and special curves. Let us study these methods briefly.

13.2.1 Tabulation

In tables, data are organized in columns and rows. They are devices to present masses of data in simple format. A table can be simple or complex depending upon the number and type of measurements. When designing tables for any reason, there are certain general principles to be considered.

(a) The tables should be numbered. For example: Table 1, Table 2, etc.
(b) The title must be brief and explanatory.
(c) The headings of columns or rows should be clear and concise.
(d) The data must be presented according to the size or importance in ascending or descending order whenever possible.
(e) If percentages or averages are to be compared, they should be placed as clearly as possible.
(f) No table should be too large.
(g) Vertical arrangement of data is better than horizontal arrangement because most people find it easier to read data from top to bottom than left to right.
(h) Footnotes may be given whenever necessary, providing explanatory notes or additional information. An example is Table 13.1.

13.2.2 Charts and Diagrams

These are used to represent simple statistical data in easily understandable format. Diagrams are better retained in memory than statistical tables. On the other hand, they have the problem of losing the details of original data because of their simplicity. Whenever we want the real study and detailed information, we have to go back to the original data.

Table 13.1 Information about Defects in a Worksite

Operator ID	Number of Defects	Percentage	Last Week
Abdul	281	8%	8%
William	301	8%	9%
Antony	104	9%	10%
Selva	403	10%	10%
Peter	502	12%	13%
Christine	585	12%	11%
Rahuman	602	13%	11%
Gorge	596	13%	12%
V S Singh	625	15%	14%

Note 1: This information is obtained from our production database management system. Further information is available from programers.

Note 2: This information is only for management personnel and should not be displayed in worksite for any reason.

(a) Bar Charts

They are merely a way of presenting a set of numbers by the length of a bar. The length of the bar is proportional to the magnitude to be represented. They are easily prepared and values are compared visually. Pareto chart is also a type of bar chart. Figure 13.1 gives you an example of bar chart.

(b) Histogram

It is a pictorial diagram of frequency distribution. It consists of a series of blocks. The class intervals are given along the horizontal axis and the frequency along

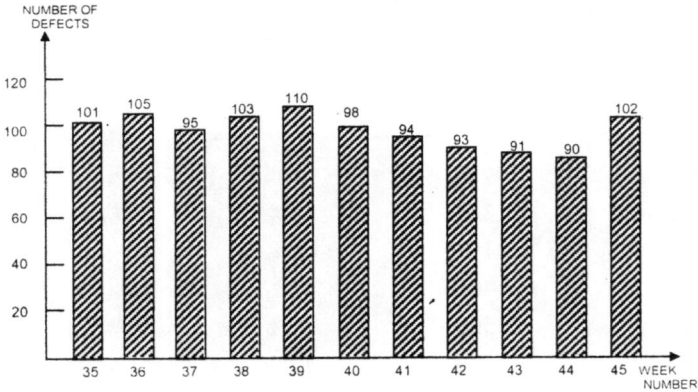

Fig. 13.1 Bar Charts

the vertical axis. The area of each block or rectangle is proportional to the frequency. Figure 13.2 gives an example of histogram and frequency polygon, which is described below.

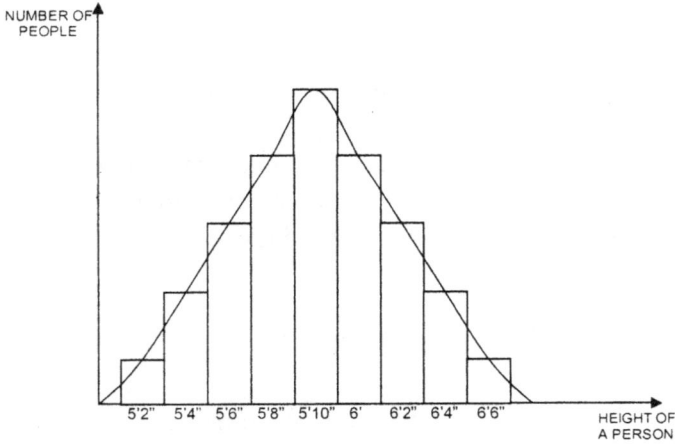

Fig. 13.2 Histogram and Frequency Polygon

Frequency Polygon

Frequency distribution may also be represented diagrammatically by a frequency polygon. It is obtained by joining the midpoints of the histogram blocks.

(c) Pie Charts

Instead of comparing the length of a bar, the areas of segments of a circle are compared. The area of each segment depends upon the angle. It is often necessary to indicate the percentage in the segments, as sometimes it may not be virtually so easy to compare areas of segments.

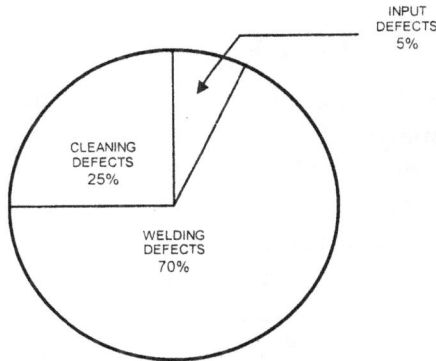

Fig. 13.3 Pie Chart

(d) Pictograms

Pictograms are a popular method of presenting data to the "man in the street" and to those who cannot understand orthodox charts. Small pictures or symbols are used to present the data. For example, a picture of a defective item to represent number of defects produced each week.

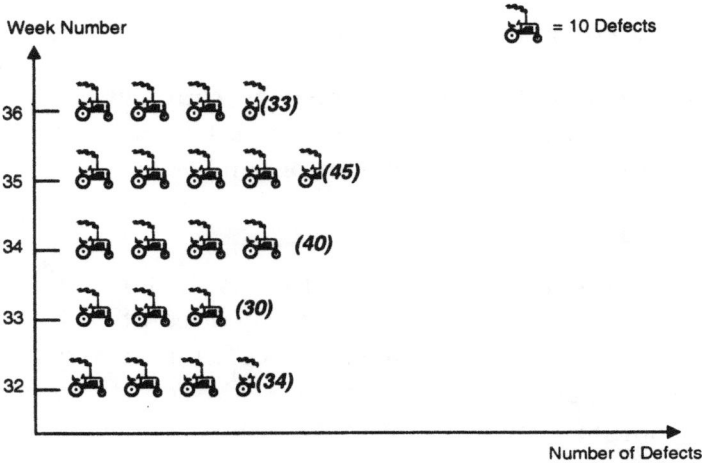

Fig. 13.4 Pictogram

13.3 STATISTICAL AVERAGES

Averages are another type of statistical indices which help us to analyze data. By the word *average* we mean a value in the distribution around which the other values are distributed. It gives us a general picture of central value. There are several kinds of averages of which the most commonly used are: (1) arithmetic mean, (2) median, and (3) mode.

(a) Arithmetic Mean

The arithmetic mean is widely used in statistical calculation. It is sometimes simply called *mean*. To obtain the mean, the individual observations are first added together, and then divided by the number of observations. The advantage of the mean is that it is easy to calculate and understand. The disadvantage is that sometimes it may be influenced by abnormal values in the distribution. However, arithmetic mean is by far the most commonly used statistical average.

(b) Median

The median is an average of a different kind which does not depend upon the total and number of items. To obtain the median, the data is first arranged in an ascending or descending order of magnitude, and then the value of the middle observation is located, which is called the *median*. When there are even a number of values and middle numbers tend to be two values, then the median is worked out by taking the average of the two middle values.

(c) Mode

The mode is the commonly conserving value in a distribution of data. It is the most frequent item or the most 'fashionable' value in a series of observations. The advantages of mode are that it is easy to understand and is not affected by the extreme items. The disadvantages are that the exact location is often uncertain and is often not clearly defined. Therefore, mode is not used very often in statistical practice.

Now let us see one example to understand these averages. The following values present the number of defects produced in a worksite in different weeks.

Week Number	31	32	33	34	35	36	37	38	39	40
Number of Defects	91	98	97	91	95	285	98	91	92	95

Here the mean will be

$$= (91+98+97+91+95+285+98+91+92+95)/10$$

$$= 113.3$$

Median value = 91,91,91,92,95,95,98,98,98,285

　　　　　　= (95+95)/2

　　　　　　= 95

The mode will be　91—111　occurs thrice

　　　　　　　　　92—1　　occurs once

　　　　　　　　　95—11　occurs twice

　　　　　　　　　97—1　　occurs once

　　　　　　　　　98—11　occurs twice

　　　　　　　　　285—1　occurs once

Most frequently occurring value that is 91.

This example helps us to understand the deficiency of mean and the mode.

13.4 SAMPLING

Another statistical technique used in analyzing the data is sampling. As explained in Chapter Twelve, when a larger proportion of individuals or items or units have to be studied we take a sample. It is easier and more economical to study the sample than the whole population or universe. In the meantime, there is a risk of alterations from actual results in the findings as a result of sampling. So great care should be taken in obtaining a sample. We have to make sure that the sample group or people or items included in the sample have the same features and problems as the whole population to be studied.

Sampling Frame

Once the universe or population need to be studied has been defined, a sampling frame must be prepared. A sampling frame is a listing of all the members of the population or universe from which the sample is to be drawn. The accuracy and completeness of the sampling frame influences the quality of the sample drawn from it.

13.4.1 Sampling Methods

Now let us see what methods are available to select a good sample from our population or universe.

(a) Simple Random Sampling

This is done by assigning a number to each of the units (the individuals or households) in the sampling frame. A table of random number is then used (see Appendix A) to determine which units are to be included in the sample. Random numbers are a haphazard collection of certain numbers, arranged in a cunning manner to eliminate personal selection of unconscious bias in taking out the sample. When you are selecting a number from random numbers, first you have to select a number by closing your eyes and touching the table with one finger. Then you have to quickly go straight downwards to the next line from top to bottom. Whenever one number is not appropriate—say you study a population of 50 people the number is 66 or the selected person numbered 45 is not accessible—then the next number is selected for the study. In the same way the sample is drawn in a way that each unit has an equal chance of being drawn in the sample.

(b) Systematic Random Sampling

This is done by picking every 5th or 10th unit at regular intervals. For example, to carry out a checking in a production line you select every 10th item for checking. But here the first number can be selected randomly for each day or each shift of work. Say the first number selected is 5, then the next numbers will be 15, 25, 35 and so on. Even though it is not so accurate as simple random sample, it has the advantage of being easy to follow and convenient in many instances.

(c) Stratified Random Sampling

The sample is deliberately drawn in a systematic way so that each portion of the sample represents a corresponding stratum of the universe. When we understand that there are different groups in our population and these groups are not equally distributed in the population, we follow this technique. Examples for such groups are religious, cultural or age groups. Here a separate sampling frame is drawn for each group and then members are selected for the sample group by simple random sampling.

(d) Cluster Random Sampling

This technique is more or less similar to stratified random sampling but the grouping is done from the geographical point of view. Here the population is divided into groups containing equal number of people. Sampling frame is drawn for each group separately. Then the sampling is done for each group by simple random sampling.

In addition to the above sampling techniques, we can also use complicated techniques by following two or three techniques at the same time in large studies. One example for such technique can be cluster stratified random sampling. Here, what we are supposed to do is first decide the population into clusters, again into different status, then do the simple random sampling. International agencies like WHO try to follow such techniques when conducting big research projects.

13.4.2 Sampling Errors

Even though we take several precautions against errors during sampling techniques, errors still occur in our studies. It can be explained in the following way. If you take repeated samples from the same population the results obtained from one sample will differ, to some extent, from the results from another sample. This type of variation from one sample to another is called *sampling error*. It occurs because data were gathered from a sample rather than from the entire population of concern.

In addition to this error due to sampling we can have non-sampling errors in our studies. These errors occur due to inadequately calibrated instruments, due to observation variation, as well as incomplete coverage achieved in explaining the subject's selected and conceptual errors.

In addition to the above errors, we can also make simple mistakes like following in our studies. For example, you are studying 100 products for mistake and you decide to do 10 per cent sampling. So you select 10 items and find out one item is defective. It means that there is the possibility of nine more defective items in the unstudied population. So when you want to record defective goods you have to say 10 items. But in some places they try to take it as 1 and try to be happy. It can be a terrible mistake and can totally mislead you.

In statistics there are ways to calculate the above errors and to find out the significance of studies we are doing. Whenever you are planning for a big study with sampling technique, you should study and utilize such techniques or get help from a professional statistician.

13.5 NORMAL DISTRIBUTION

The normal distribution or 'normal curve' is an important concept in statistical theory. Let us suppose we collect the height of a very large number of people and make a frequency distribution with narrow class intervals, we will get a smooth, symmetrical curve like Figure 13.5. Such a curve is called a *normal distribution* or *normal curve*. The shape of the curve will depend upon the number and nature of observations.

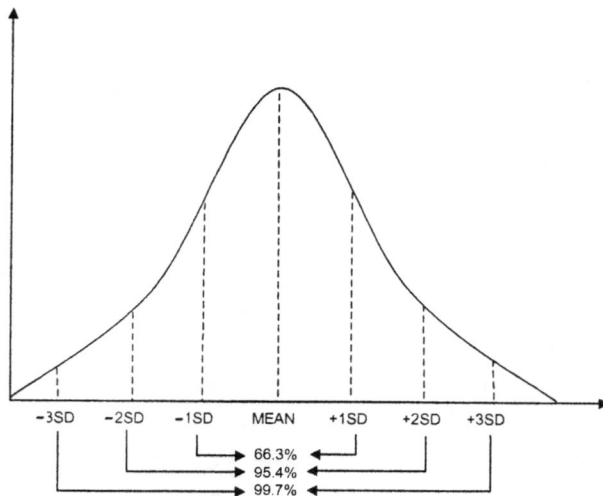

Fig. 13.5 Normal Curve

One important concept in normal curve is standard deviation. What do we mean by *standard deviation?* Earlier we have seen about mean that is the normal average that we are using in our everyday life. If we take a number of observations except for a few observations, which will be exactly the same as the mean, every other one will deviate by a value from the mean. For example, take three numbers: 5, 7 and 9. Here the mean or average will be (5+7+9)/3, that is 7. Here except for the middle number the other two numbers 5 and 9 will deviate from the mean by 2 on either side. The average of these deviations is called *mean deviation*. Here (2+2)/3 that is 1.33 is mean deviation.

Standard deviation is a little more complicated. To find out standard deviation you have to follow the following steps:

(a) First of all, take the deviation of each value from the arithmetic mean.
(b) Then square each deviation.
(c) Add up the squared deviations.
(d) Divide the result by the number of observations (if the number of observation is less that 30, then n-1).
(e) Then take the square root, which gives the standard deviation.

The above concepts can be more clearly explained in the following example.

Operator ID	Number of Defects	Arithmetic Mean	Deviation from Mean	Square of Deviations
001	83	81	2	4
002	75	81	−6	36
007	81	81	0	—
009	75	81	−2	4
021	71	81	−10	100
032	95	81	14	196
055	75	81	−6	36
072	77	81	−4	16
127	84	81	3	9
238	90	81	9	81
Total	810		56 (ignore '+' and '−' signs) 482	

Mean   = 810/10
                = 81

Mean Deviation = 56/10
                = 5.6

Standard Deviation = 482/(10–1) = 482/9 = 53.55
                    = 7.31

Basically, a standard deviation is an abstract number; it gives us an idea of the spread of the dispersion; the larger the standard deviation, the greater the dispersion of values about the mean. In a normal curve, standard deviation helps us as follows.

(a) The area between one standard deviation on either side of the mean will include approximately 68 per cent of the values in a distribution.

(b) The area between two standard deviations on either side of the mean will cover approximately 95 per cent of the values.

(c) The area between three standard deviations on either side of the mean will cover approximately 99.7 per cent of the values.

This knowledge about standard deviation helps us to find out whether any specific value deviates significantly from the mean. Even though there are different opinions, usually any value, which lies above 2 standard deviation, is considered as significantly different. One important point we have to remember here is in most instances deviation on one side is considered as undesirable while deviation to other side will be desirable.

Chapter Fourteen

UNDERSTANDING ABOUT COMPUTERS

14.1 INTRODUCTION TO COMPUTERS

The most frequent word used in business world today may be *computers*. Computers are being used almost in every function of management. They help in marketing, are used in accounting, for planning and organizing and so on. Even though installing and maintaining a computer system is a computer engineer's job, it is better for managers to have an understanding of their capacity and limitations so that we can use them in our work more efficiently.

14.1.1 Hardware

To own a computer, you need two types of components. First one is known as *hardware* and other one is known as *software*. The *hardware* includes all the physical components of computers. Video display unit, a TV screen-like part; keyboard, a typewriter-like part; system unit, a box-like part where hard drive, floppy disk drive and all-important chips are held together and every other physical component joined to the computer are called *hardware*. If you join all of these components properly, plug to electricity and try to turn on the computer you may only see a blank TV screen or a simple line asking to insert the boot disk. If you want to run your computer, you need another important component called *software*. A detailed understanding of software available in the market is important for a manager. Let us see them in more detail.

14.1.2 Software[17]

When you buy a computer, in addition to the hardware you have received, you will also be supplied with some disks, which are important for its functions. In these disks information is stored in a format which can be read by the computers. This information constitutes instructions for the computer to perform each task. After assembling the computer, when you start it for first time, you have to insert these disks in the proper order into disk drives with necessary instructions. Usually these programs will be stored to your hard disk at first instance, and later your computer will start and work without these disks. Software can be grouped into three major categories according to their function.

Operating System

These are the basic and important instructions necessary for the functions of a computer. Operating system will connect and control different devices like video display unit, mouse, printer and keyboard to the main system. In addition, the operating system will regulate the information to be stored in the computer. Without installing an operating system, you cannot go any further in using the computer. Commonly used operating systems are MS-DOS, WINDOWS, UNIX, SUN operating system, etc.

Compiler Software

Actually computers are not capable of understanding languages talked by humans. They only understand and communicate with each part by electronic signals, which are known as machine language. But you know that the instructions we are giving to the computers from keyboard or by mouse on screen are in one of the languages we commonly speak and understand. The software that helps the computer to understand the instruction is a compiler. It works as translator and translates the instruction from human language to machine language and from machine language to human language. Whenever you try to install a program on your computer the compiler will be installed automatically and starts to work as translator between the program and the hardware. Examples for compiler software are C compiler for programs written in C language, Pascal compiler for programs written in Pascal language.

Application Software

This is the most important part for us. It constitutes the programs written to perform certain tasks for the users. It may be typing a letter, billing in a counter or accounting and so on. There are different kinds for different purposes. Most commonly used application software are word processors, spreadsheets, presentation software and DBMS.

- Word processors are used for typing, editing and printing simple office letters to small booklets. Example for word processors are Word Perfect, Word and Microsoft Word.

- Spreadsheets are used to state mainly numerical data in the form of rows and columns. They allow you to perform detailed analysis and calculations on numerical data. Some of the popular spreadsheet packages are Lotus 1-2-3, Quattro Pro and MS Excel.
- Presentation software is used to create professional quality presentations, which can be reproduced on transparency paper, 35 mm slides, and photo print and on screen presentations. Example of presentations software is MS Power Point.
- Database Management Systems [DBMS] used to store not only numerical data but data in different formats. In DBMS you can store text, numbers, dates, pictures, sound and video images and so on. Examples of DBMS are FoxPro, Clipper, MS Access and Oracle.

The four types of software discussed above are collectively called *office packages* because they are used for better functions of office not only in business but also in every other type of organization. Even though the first three—word processors, spreadsheet and presentation software—help us in our business, the last one—Database Management Systems is the most important from the viewpoint of quality management. We have studied that quality management is an information based management system. Only DBMS can give us a convenient software to store and analyze different types of data. Before looking into DBMS in more detail, let us see what are the important functions of a computer.

14.2 FUNCTIONS OF A COMPUTER

Today computers help mankind in many different ways, from running our washing machines to helping to launch and maintain satellites. So obviously computers have to perform many different functions. At least for our learning purpose, it may be possible for us to group these functions in the following categories.

1. Repetition

Computers are capable of doing repetitive functions very accurately in high speed. It may be printing a letter again and again or controlling a machine which does things repeatedly. When humans are asked to do such a job, it not only causes fatigue but also results in more errors as they proceed. But computers can do such tasks with very good diligence.

2. Arithmetic Calculations

Another important function computers can perform for us is arithmetic calculations. This may be performed by small calculators for simple arithmetic or by a super computer for weather forecast. Computers are capable of doing arithmetic calculations at high speed with better accuracy.

3. Information Management

This is the most important function computers are performing from quality management point of view. Computers are capable of storing many different kinds of information and allow to retrieve this information for further use in whatever format we like. As we studied earlier, the software we use for information management system is Database Management System. When these DBMS follow certain standards, rules and regulations, they are known as Relational Data Base Management System.

4. Decision-Making

Even though computers are capable of doing the above functions on a more superior level than human beings, when it come to decision-making function, computers are lying much further back than the human brain. Several attempts have been made to use computers in decision-making būt unfortunately they are only capable up to the level they are instructed. Even a slightly different situation makes computers either produce erroneous results or abandon the task altogether. It is difficult to say whether it is good or bad that computers do not have the capability of decision-making. At least for the time being, it is better to leave this task to human intelligence.

14.3 DATABASE MANAGEMENT SYSTEM[17, 18]

As we have seen earlier, it is the most important subject a quality management person likes to know in computer science. A Database Management System is essentially a collection of interrelated data and a set of programs to access this data. Usually DBMS offers the following services.

- Data Definition: It is a method of defining data types that need to be stored.
- Data Maintenance: It checks whether each record has fields containing all information.

- Data Manipulation: This allows data in the database to be inserted, updated, deleted and sorted.
- Data Display: This helps in viewing data.
- Data Integrity: This ensures accuracy of the data.

When a DBMS meets certain standards of American National Standard Institution [ANSI] it is called Relational DBMS [RDBMS]. An RDBMS can support a common computer language called *structured quarry language* [SQL]. With the help of SQL you can create a database, maintain data in it and revise necessary information whenever you need. Examples of RDBMS are Oracle, Sybase, SQL Server, DB2, etc.

A database is made up of data and associated objects. Database objects include tables, queries, forms and reports. Let us study these database objects in some more detail.

14.3.1 Tables

The information stored in a database is in the form of one or more tables. The tables are created in the format of rows and columns. Each table in a database focuses on one different type of information. There will be one table for information about the process, another table for information about the machines, another table for information about customers and so on. Table 14.1 gives you a possible table of information about some machines.

Each table is divided into several rows and columns. Each row contains information about different machines. A single row with all of its information is called a *record*. Fields in a table are the columns of

Table 14.1 Table of Machines

Machine ID	Type	Manufacturer	Date of Purchase
9801	Cutter	Tata	Jan 1998
9802	Cutter	Yamaha	Jan 1998
9803	Driller	Yamaha	Feb 1998

information. For example in Table 14.1 the third field from left field contains information about the manufacturer. So, fields store a particular type of information. Every specific piece of information in a table is known as a value. Thus TATA is a value, Jan 1998 is a value, and so on.

14.3.2 Queries

Queries are used to extract information from a database. A query can select a group of records that fulfill certain conditions with specified fields. An example of a query is when you want to see the list of machines produced by YAMAHA company. The Result of such query on Table 14.1 may be as in Table 14.2.

Table 14.2 Results of Query to select Information about YAMAHA Machine

Machine ID	Type	Manufacturer	Date of Purchase
9802	Cutter	YAMAHA	Jan 1998
9803	Driller	YAMAHA	Feb 1998

Out of the four database objects we see here that a good understanding about queries will help quality management persons to analyze information about defects. In Section 14.4, we will see some simple queries on a sample database. If you get a chance to learn about DBMS and queries, it will certainly help you in your work.

14.3.3 Forms

Forms help users to enter information into a database table in an easy and accurate manner. More than entering data into the tables, you can also change, delete or view database records. You can use data-entry forms to restrict access to certain fields within a table. You can also use these forms to check the validity of the data before it is accepted into the database. For example you can ensure that "manufacturer" fields are not left blank; "data of purchase" is entered in month/year format. It is also possible to allow selective display of certain fields within the given table. By displaying selected fields, you can limit a users' access to sensitive data.

14.3.4 Reports

Reports present your data in a printed format. You can create different types of reports with a DBMS. For example, your report can list all the records in a given table such as a list of all machines. You can even generate a report that lists only selective records, such as machines, purchased in January 1998. You can do this by incorporating a query within the report. Your reports

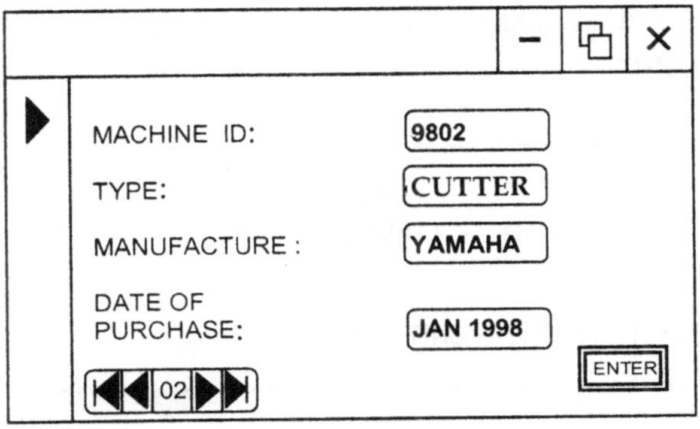

Fig. 14.1 A Sample Form

can also combine multiple tables to present complex relationships among different sets of data. When you design your database, remember the information that you will need in the future. Doing so ensures that all the information you require in your reports is easily available. Usually DBMS have facility of printing reports as figures or graphics; for example, pareto charts, pie charts and so on.

Now we can see a sample database, which can be created for a small department quality management system.

14.4 QUALITY MANAGEMENT DATABASE[19]

The following is a sample database of a quality management system for a small department. Imagine a department which takes two inputs, connector and terminal. They are being joined together by doing two different processes, namely cleaning and welding, and the output is called *Adopter*.

A possible checksheet for such a department may be as in Figure 14.2.

XXXX COMPANY
ADOPTER DEPARTMENT
QUALITY CHECK SHEET

QUALITY CHECKING UNIT NO: 0 7

PRODUCT ID: 9833431

CONNECTOR ID: 9831031   TERMINAL ID: 9824321

CLEANING
OPERATOR ID [   ]   STATION NO [   ]

HUMIDITY [   ]   DATE [   ]   SHIFT [   ]

WELDING
OPERATOR ID [   ]   MACHINE NO [   ]

ROOM TEMP [   ]   DATE [   ]   SHIFT [   ]

QUALITY CHECKING

QUALITY
CHECKER ID [   ]

	DEFECT	INTENSITY
CLEANING DEFECT		
WELDING DEFECT		

NON-CONFORMANCE NEED TO BE REPORTED

· CLEANING   **WELDING**
NO DEFECTS : 0   NO DEFECTS : 0
ACCEPTABLE DEFECTS: 1   ACCEPTABLE DEFECTS :· 1
REJECTABLE DEFECTS : 2   REJECTABLE DEFECTS : 2

Fig. 14.2 Sample Checksheet

Usually all the information in the above checksheet is entered in single table. But such table can be connected to several different tables by different ID numbers we are entering here. How to create tables, how to create necessary forms and reports is beyond the scope of this study. You can create such database with somebody's help in MS Access or any other DBMS, which can support quarry language.

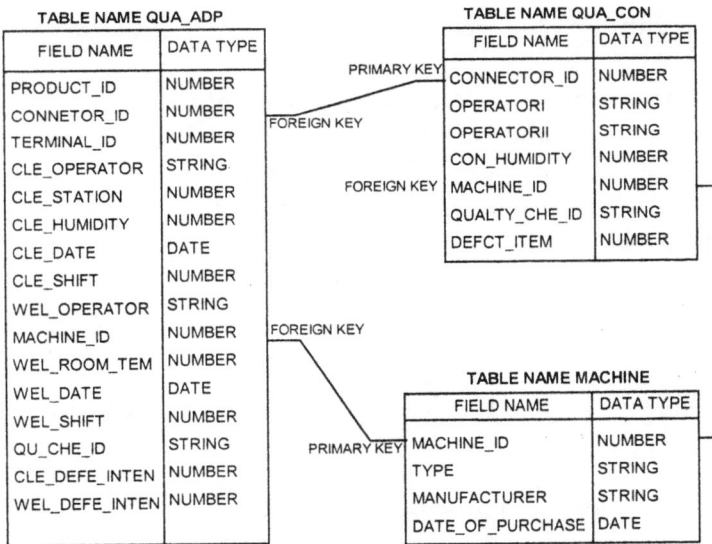

TABLE NAME QUA_ADP

FIELD NAME	DATA TYPE
PRODUCT_ID	NUMBER
CONNETOR_ID	NUMBER
TERMINAL_ID	NUMBER
CLE_OPERATOR	STRING
CLE_STATION	NUMBER
CLE_HUMIDITY	NUMBER
CLE_DATE	DATE
CLE_SHIFT	NUMBER
WEL_OPERATOR	STRING
MACHINE_ID	NUMBER
WEL_ROOM_TEM	NUMBER
WEL_DATE	DATE
WEL_SHIFT	NUMBER
QU_CHE_ID	STRING
CLE_DEFE_INTEN	NUMBER
WEL_DEFE_INTEN	NUMBER

TABLE NAME QUA_CON

FIELD NAME	DATA TYPE
CONNECTOR_ID	NUMBER
OPERATORI	STRING
OPERATORII	STRING
CON_HUMIDITY	NUMBER
MACHINE_ID	NUMBER
QUALTY_CHE_ID	STRING
DEFCT_ITEM	NUMBER

PRIMARY KEY

FOREIGN KEY

FOREIGN KEY

FOREIGN KEY

PRIMARY KEY

TABLE NAME MACHINE

FIELD NAME	DATA TYPE
MACHINE_ID	NUMBER
TYPE	STRING
MANUFACTURER	STRING
DATE_OF_PURCHASE	DATE

Fig. 14.3 Sample Table Structure and Relations

You can see a sample set of data for the 3 tables above in Appendix B. Now let us see how to retrieve information from tables above to identify causes of problems.

Earlier we studied about structured query language. There are different commands in SQL to create tables and to insert and maintain data in it. But an important

SQL command we need to know is command to retrieve information. The word used here as command is SELECT. Let us see more detail about this select command.

When you want to retrieve information from a database, you have to give select query as follows.

Select {name of field you want to see} from {name of tables from where you want to select fields} where {conditions for records, which need to be selected};

Here sometimes we don't need to use 'where'.

Let us see some examples of queries which can select information from our sample database.

(a) Let us begin with the simplest query—Retrieve all Fields from Table Machine.

Select *
from MACHINE;

Here "*" used to mention all fields and all SQL commands will end with ";".

Such query will give you whole table of Machine
How to select whole table QUE_CON?

(b) How to select specific fields from a table with specific conditions for records need to be displayed.

Give Product ID and Name of cleaning operators for products having rejectable cleaning defects.

Select PRODUCT_ID, CLE_OPERATOR
from QUA_ADD
where CLE_DEFE_INTEN = 2;

Such query will give you product ID and name of the cleaning operator of products, which have rejectable defects. Such query may help you find whether the defects are associated with any specific person who may need further training.

In such instances selecting all fields may be more valuable as it may give you any hidden cause of the problem.

(c) How to select information about defects in product, which are produced when humidity is above 60.0.

    Select *
    from QUA_ADP
    where CLE_HUMIDITY > 60.0;

This query will give you all information about the products, which are produced when humidity is above 60%.

(d) We want to see the following fields from two tables. From QUA_ADP table we want to see PRODUCT_ID, MACHINE_ID and WEL_DEFE_ INTEN and from Machine table we want to see MACHINE_ID, TYPE, MANUFACTURER and DATA_OF_PURCHASE of machine used in production of each item. How to do this? How to retrieve data from two different tables?

    Select QUA_ADP.PRODUCT_ID, QUA_ADP. MACHINE_ID, _ QUA_ADP.WEL_DEFE_INTEN, MACHINE.*
    from QUA_ADP, MACHINE
    where QUA_ADP.MACHINE_ID = MACHINE. MACHINE_ID;

(e) We have a suspicion that the defects in welding area of Adaptor Department may be due to some factors in Connector Department. How to know whether there is any relation between welding defects and connector department. We can select all the fields from tables QUA_ADP and QUA_CON with following query.

> Select QUA_ADP.*, QUA_CON.*
> from QUA_ADP, QUA_CON
> where QUA_ADP.CONNECTOR_ID = QUA_CON.
> CONNECTOR_ID, and WEL_DEFE_ INTEN = 2;

The five querries discussed here will give you some understanding about query language. But query language is much more powerful than this. A good software programer can give you much more complicated selection of data which may be useful in finding out the causes of defects.

14.5 CONCLUSION

This concludes our discussion on TQM and associated subjects. It was not the author's intention to try to bring a new management philosophy or new management idea through this book. The intention was to present today's most needed management knowledge in simple English with possible examples and explanations from physiological, psychological and social concepts. Middle managers, supervisory people and professionals working in industry and service sector will find this most useful to them.

RANDOM NUMBERS

Tables in this section give you a set of random numbers. When you want to select random numbers, first you have to close your eyes and touch the table with one finger to select a number. If you have selected the intersection of column 9 and row 16, then the number is "1". Then find out how many digits there are in your total population figure. If the total population is 95, then it consists of two digits. If it is 3755, then it consists of four digits. You have to include columns on the right hand side of your selected column to accommodate all digits. Say, your total population consists of two digits, then one more column is included, that is 10. After doing this, go straight downwards to select random numbers.

For example, you are asked to check the quality of a batch of 60 products. The procedure says 10 per cent sampling has to be done. So you have to select 6 items for quality checking. As we saw earlier you have to select 6 items from the batch and have to do the quality checking. Say, you have selected "1" from the intersection of column 9 and row 16. Your total population consists of two digits. So include column 10 for your selection. Record the first number. It is "10". So you have to do quality checking on the 10th product

The following figures give you a set of random numbers.

Row	1	2	3	4	5	6	7	8	9	10	11	12	13	14	15	16	17	18	19
1	9	8	9	6	9	9	0	9	6	3	2	3	3	8	6	8	4	4	2
2	3	5	6	1	7	4	1	3	2	6	8	6	0	4	7	5	2	0	3
3	4	0	6	1	6	9	6	1	5	9	5	4	5	4	8	6	7	4	0
4	6	5	6	3	1	6	8	6	7	2	0	7	2	3	2	1	5	0	9
5	2	4	9	7	9	1	0	3	9	6	7	4	1	5	4	9	6	9	8
6	7	6	1	2	7	5	6	9	4	8	4	2	8	5	2	4	1	8	0
7	8	2	1	3	4	7	4	6	3	0	7	5	0	9	2	9	0	6	1
8	6	9	5	6	5	6	0	9	0	7	7	1	4	1	8	3	1	9	3
9	7	2	1	9	9	8	0	1	6	1	6	2	3	6	9	5	5	8	4
10	2	9	0	7	3	0	8	9	6	3	3	8	5	5	6	5	2	0	9
11	9	3	5	4	5	7	4	0	3	0	1	0	4	3	3	9	5	3	2
12	9	7	5	7	9	4	8	6	8	7	6	1	6	8	2	5	5	5	3
13	4	1	7	8	6	8	1	0	5	8	8	6	1	6	8	2	9	0	4
14	5	0	8	3	3	4	5	4	4	2	5	3	0	4	9	6	1	2	3
15	3	5	0	2	9	4	1	0	0	3	9	0	5	8	6	0	9	9	6
16	0	3	8	2	3	5	1	0	1	0	6	8	5	2	4	8	0	3	8
17	1	7	2	9	1	2	7	8	4	7	0	3	3	1	5	8	2	7	3
18	5	0	5	7	9	5	8	7	8	9	3	5	3	4	4	6	1	1	3
19	7	7	3	3	5	3	6	1	3	2	8	5	4	1	4	8	3	9	0
20	1	0	9	1	3	8	2	5	3	0	3	8	0	9	3	3	0	4	5
21	1	3	8	5	1	8	5	9	4	1	9	3	9	3	6	5	9	8	4
22	8	6	4	7	8	7	5	9	4	1	9	3	9	3	6	5	9	8	4
23	0	6	9	6	5	1	0	3	2	6	7	7	4	9	6	0	3	4	0
24	7	6	7	4	7	0	8	3	8	7	3	2	5	1	2	4	2	9	7
25	3	2	3	8	1	3	1	8	7	4	5	9	0	0	2	4	1	2	1
26	9	2	1	6	4	2	3	8	7	6	2	6	2	6	4	8	1	0	1
27	3	7	4	2	2	8	1	7	8	0	6	0	0	0	3	2	2	9	7
28	0	7	8	0	8	5	1	5	2	6	5	8	7	5	3	0	5	9	6
29	7	4	2	3	3	2	6	0	0	6	5	2	2	3	6	3	9	0	4
30	1	8	2	7	5	9	5	3	6	5	2	9	9	1	1	7	3	4	3
31	4	3	1	8	7	0	6	0	8	6	5	0	1	0	4	0	6	1	5
32	8	5	8	0	6	1	4	1	2	0	4	4	1	4	7	6	3	5	1
33	4	5	8	5	0	4	5	8	3	9	2	8	7	8	9	0	8	4	3
34	5	0	2	5	4	9	2	2	1	1	0	0	5	4	8	7	6	4	0
35	0	8	1	7	0	6	3	3	4	7	6	2	6	8	9	3	4	1	4
36	2	5	9	3	4	6	0	7	5	2	0	0	9	6	0	8	2	2	5
37	2	1	3	1	3	7	8	9	8	4	9	3	8	0	2	2	1	8	1
38	3	8	8	6	8	.5	1	3	3	4	6	7	2	6	3	4	8	6	7
39	0	9	9	8	5	9	8	4	4	2	2	1	1	0	1	7	6	1	3
40	2	2	3	5	3	9	7	4	4	2	1	4	0	5	8	2	3	0	8

								Column Number													
20	21	22	23	24	25	26	27	28	29	30	31	32	33	34	35	36	37	38	39	40	Row
0	9	7	1	1	9	1	2	7	3	5	1	8	4	0	4	1	0	6	0	3	1
8	3	7	7	9	1	4	9	9	5	9	2	0	1	6	1	2	6	6	7	0	2
2	5	6	3	7	8	3	3	8	4	3	9	3	9	0	0	9	8	3	5	2	3
4	7	0	8	6	6	5	9	6	2	7	3	5	9	0	1	8	0	9	6	9	4
0	9	8	7	3	5	6	8	8	1	2	0	2	3	2	6	4	3	1	9	7	5
5	1	8	8	4	7	0	1	7	6	8	2	1	6	3	2	1	8	1	8	3	6
1	3	7	8	6	9	5	4	1	7	3	8	7	1	5	6	5	6	4	3	6	7
5	9	0	1	5	2	8	6	5	5	7	8	1	8	7	1	2	4	0	4	1	8
2	2	5	5	2	1	8	6	9	8	9	8	0	5	8	9	9	4	1	3	4	9
1	3	4	2	8	5	0	7	9	8	4	3	5	8	0	9	4	6	6	0	5	10
2	6	8	6	6	4	7	1	5	1	6	4	6	7	6	0	8	7	3	5	2	11
8	6	0	1	4	2	9	8	6	8	0	7	6	5	1	9	1	3	7	0	3	12
9	5	7	0	9	8	7	6	9	0	6	5	4	0	3	6	5	6	3	5	0	13
2	2	3	4	7	8	0	2	0	8	0	3	4	9	2	5	7	7	8	6	4	14
2	4	6	1	0	5	0	6	1	4	9	4	7	3	9	1	7	6	4	5	8	15
6	3	4	8	1	6	9	5	6	2	0	4	6	1	6	8	1	9	9	1	1	16
9	0	5	1	3	6	1	9	5	4	1	2	5	4	2	9	5	6	2	4	0	17
3	6	7	0	3	5	3	7	4	1	7	5	4	8	3	7	4	8	5	7	2	18
4	3	6	6	3	6	3	0	0	9	4	2	2	5	1	8	9	5	1	9	7	19
1	0	6	9	0	2	7	3	9	8	4	0	6	9	8	2	3	2	8	0	4	20
9	1	3	5	7	9	6	2	4	3	4	6	4	9	1	3	1	7	5	2	2	21
6	4	2	2	2	1	4	5	2	2	8	3	2	1	2	6	6	0	1	8	9	22
7	2	6	9	0	7	5	3	2	5	6	2	7	6	3	8	1	4	1	5	1	23
8	2	8	2	4	4	4	2	9	1	9	8	3	4	4	1	0	4	6	9	6	24
7	3	1	4	3	0	4	7	1	3	7	4	8	6	7	3	2	6	6	2	0	25
0	6	4	5	8	3	1	4	8	1	8	3	1	6	4	3	0	2	8	7	3	26
4	2	2	8	3	2	1	9	3	0	1	7	5	9	0	9	1	2	5	8	2	27
2	9	8	7	2	0	6	4	0	2	7	1	3	1	6	8	7	0	9	2	5	28
0	8	0	5	6	8	2	4	3	6	1	3	5	2	3	5	9	8	6	2	1	29
0	1	7	6	1	5	7	9	0	3	5	3	4	2	4	8	5	6	4	0	6	30
5	1	9	8	5	2	4	5	1	7	5	3	2	4	6	7	9	9	6	7	2	31
0	3	6	6	3	7	8	6	9	7	2	8	9	0	7	2	9	4	0	8	6	32
5	0	0	0	2	0	8	9	0	1	0	6	2	0	4	6	9	6	5	4	9	33
1	9	4	4	2	6	4	2	4	1	0	2	7	9	6	8	7	5	6	9	3	34
0	0	5	3	8	3	2	7	5	0	4	7	6	4	6	3	0	4	7	5	3	35
6	2	6	2	0	6	0	1	4	8	9	6	5	9	7	3	6	7	6	5	4	36
6	3	9	0	3	5	0	9	1	2	0	5	9	7	3	2	5	9	3	0	2	37
9	7	3	3	5	4	0	6	4	9	4	7	9	1	4	3	9	7	7	1	8	38
1	9	6	2	9	4	2	9	7	0	3	8	9	5	7	0	6	9	7	2	5	39
5	9	4	5	8	6	2	3	0	6	2	9	8	6	3	0	4	1	0	7	6	40

of the batch. Next numbers for quality checking are done as follows. Go straight downwards to the next number that is "47". Next one is "89" but it is not an accessible number as our batch consists of only 60 products. So go straight downward to the next number. Next is "32". Next number is "30", next is "41". We need one more number. Next is also "41" but we have already selected the item. So go one number below that is "21". In this way, we can select the numbers we want. When you end up in one set of lines you move to the next set of lines. In this example the next lines will be 11 and 12.

After selecting the items, go ahead with the quality checking. If you find out 1 product is defective, you have to record the number of defective goods in the batch as 10 (1 x 10) because you are doing a 10 per cent sampling here.

A SAMPLE QUALITY DATABASE

The following database is a sample for you to practice
the examples given in Chapter Fourteen.

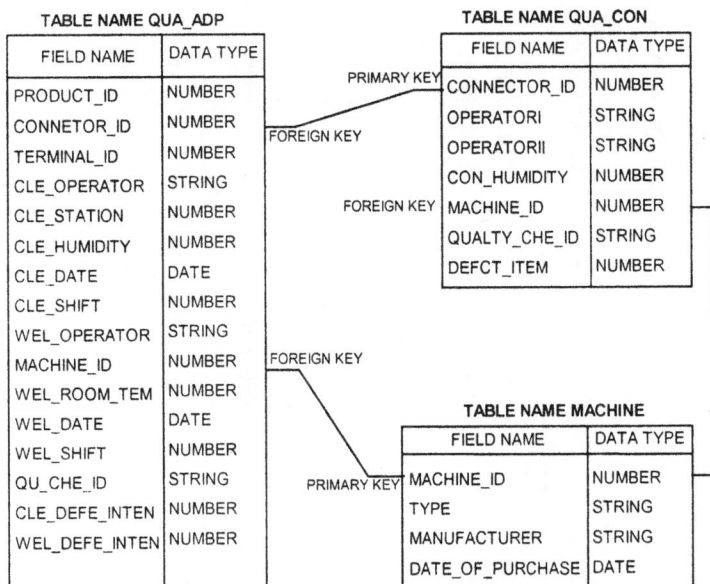

TABLE NAME QUA_ADP

FIELD NAME	DATA TYPE
PRODUCT_ID	NUMBER
CONNETOR_ID	NUMBER
TERMINAL_ID	NUMBER
CLE_OPERATOR	STRING
CLE_STATION	NUMBER
CLE_HUMIDITY	NUMBER
CLE_DATE	DATE
CLE_SHIFT	NUMBER
WEL_OPERATOR	STRING
MACHINE_ID	NUMBER
WEL_ROOM_TEM	NUMBER
WEL_DATE	DATE
WEL_SHIFT	NUMBER
QU_CHE_ID	STRING
CLE_DEFE_INTEN	NUMBER
WEL_DEFE_INTEN	NUMBER

TABLE NAME QUA_CON

FIELD NAME	DATA TYPE
CONNECTOR_ID	NUMBER
OPERATORI	STRING
OPERATORII	STRING
CON_HUMIDITY	NUMBER
MACHINE_ID	NUMBER
QUALTY_CHE_ID	STRING
DEFCT_ITEM	NUMBER

PRIMARY KEY
FOREIGN KEY
FOREIGN KEY
FOREIGN KEY
PRIMARY KEY

TABLE NAME MACHINE

FIELD NAME	DATA TYPE
MACHINE_ID	NUMBER
TYPE	STRING
MANUFACTURER	STRING
DATE_OF_PURCHASE	DATE

Fig. 1 Sample Table Structure and Relations

Table 1 QUA_ADP

PRODUCT_ID	CONNECTOR_ID	TERMINAL_ID	CLE_OPERATOR	CLE_STATION
ADP0103001	CON0102022	TER0101125	Andrew	CLE3
ADP0103002	CON0102031	TER0101122	Andrew	CLE3
ADP0103003	CON0102034	TER0101322	Andrew	CLE3
ADP0103004	CON0102054	TER0101344	Peter	CLE4
ADP0103005	CON0102043	TER0101444	Peter	CLE4
ADP0103006	CON0102055	TER0101543	Peter	CLE3
ADP0103007	CON0102065	TER0101132	Peter	CLE3
ADP0103008	CON0102044	TER0101654	Mohamed	CLE4
ADP0103009	CON0102123	TER0101456	Woung	CLE3

CLE_HUMIDITY	CLE_DATE	CLE_SHIFT	WEL_OPERATOR	MACHINE_ID
45	01/03/2001	1	Lee	WEL9901
40	01/03/2001	2	Lee	WEL9901
60	01/03/2001	2	Lee	WEL9701
65	01/03/2001	1	Lee	WEL9701
67	01/03/2001	1	Lee	WEL9701
40	02/03/2001	3	Daniel	WEL9903
42	02/03/2001	3	Daniel	WEL9903
65	02/03/2001	3	Daniel	WEL9903
63	02/03/2001	3	Kumran	WEL9901

(Contd.)

WEL_ROOM_TEMP	WEL_DATE	WEL_SHIFT	QU_CHE_ID	CLE_DEFE_INTEN	WEL_DEFE_INTEN
30	2/3/2001	1	Barbara	01	02
29	2/3/2001	1	Barbara	00	00
32	2/3/2001	2	Barbara	01	00
25	2/3/2001	2	Ramani	00	01
27	2/3/2001	2	Ramani	02	02
28	3/3/2001	1	Ramani	01	00
30	3/3/2001	1	Tamara	00	01
32	3/3/2001	1	Tamara	01	02
34	3/3/2001	2	Tamara	00	00

Table 2 QUA_CON

CONNECTOR_ID	OPERATORI	OPERATORII	CON_HUMIDITY	MACHINE_ID	QUALITY_CHE_ID	DEFECT_ITEM
CON0102022	Sharier	S Singh	65	CON9901	Robin	00
CON0102031	Sharier	S Singh	64	CON9901	Robin	01
CON0102034	Sharier	S Singh	63	CON9901	Robin	00
CON0102054	Sharier	S Singh	65	CON9901	Robin	01
CON0102043	Nancy	Ramkee	56	CON9701	Abdulle	00
CON0102055	Nancy	Ramkee	57	CON9701	Abdulle	00
CON0102065	Nancy	Ramkee	55	CON9701	Abdulle	00
CON0102044	Victor	Ramkee	58	CON9701	Abdulle	01
CON0102123	Victor	Ramkee	57	CON9701	Abdulle	01

Table 3 Machine

MACHINE_ID	TYPE	MANUFACTURER	DATE_OF_PURCHASE
CON9901	CONNECTOR	YAMAHA	JAN 1999
CON9701	CONNECTOR	YAMAHA	JAN 1997
CON9503	CONNECTOR	TATA	FEB 1995
WEL9901	WELDER	TATA	JAN 1999
WEL9903	WELDER	YAMAHA	FEB 1999
WEL9701	WELDER	TATA	JAN 1997

EVALUATION QUESTIONNAIRE FOR TQM SYSTEM

The following questionnaire will help you access the TQM system functioning inside your organization. Answer the following questions and refer to the evaluation at the end of the questions.

1. Our management always emphasizes on the...
    (i) Quantity of production.
    (ii) Quantity and Quality of production.
    (iii) Quality of production.

2. With our products provision of regular customer communication channels (refer Section 5.4.a).
    (i) We do not provide any.
    (ii) We usually provide one way.
    (iii) We always provide at least two ways.

3. Measurement indices (refer Chapter Six).
    (i) We don't have any measurement indices for our worksite.
    (ii) We have few but not documented.
    (iii) We have well-established measurement indices for our worksite (for products and people).

4. About quality checking at worksite.
    (i)   We only check final product for quality with an AQL system.
    (ii) We have several quality checking points but we accept AQL as a better technique.
    (iii) We have several quality checking and in at least one or two places we have zero defect checking.

5. Usage of quality management tools to prepare reports and during discussions (refer Chapter Seven).
    (i)   We do not use them.
    (ii) We use a few of them.
    (iii) We regularly use most of them.

6. Common language for the company (refer Section 8.2).
    (i)   We do not have any such common identity.
    (ii) We have a common identity but we are not serious about wearing it in our worksites.
    (iii) We have a common identity, which is respected, at all levels.

7. Communication system for the company (refer Section 8.4).
    (i)   We conduct production meeting only when it is needed.
    (ii) We have a production meeting every month.
    (iii) We have a production meeting every week.

8. Suggestion system (refer Section 8.5).
    (i)   We do not have a suggestion system.

    (ii) We have a suggestion system but rarely receive useful ideas.

    (iii) We have a well-organized suggestion system and receive at least a couple of useful ideas every month.

9. About employees' motivation system (refer Chapter Nine).

    (i) We don't have any concepts explained there.

    (ii) We have a few of them.

    (iii) We have a well-organized system for every concept there.

10. About training programme (refer Chapter Ten).

    (i) We do not have any specific training program.

    (ii) We have a training and certification program but it is not a barrier for promotions.

    (iii) We have a well-organized training and certification program and promotions are given on that basis.

11. Change towards TQM (refer Section 11.2).

    (i) We do not have any organized changing program.

    (ii) We accept TQM is a program change and have a rapidly changing program for 5 years.

    (iii) We accept TQM is a cultural change and have a changing process over 15 years.

12. ˙ Quality circles (refer Section 11.2.B).
   (i)   We do not have any quality circles in our worksites.
   (ii) We have a few, but they are not organized.
   (iii) We have several organized quality circles in our worksite.

Give scoring for your answers as follows:
If answer is i score is 1.
If answer is ii score is 2.
If answer is iii score is 3.

Total up your score and refer the following tables:

Group 4A: Score 36–30: You have an organized TQM system, regular counselling and updates will keep you fit.

Group 3A: Score 29–24: You have some components of TQM system, but more effect needed for improvement.

Group 2A: Score 23–18: You have a few components of TQM system, but only serious effort can help you to make improvement.

Group 1A: Scores 17–12: Could be the next "Titanic" at any time.

REFERENCES

1. Total Quality Management

Crosby, Philip B., *Quality is Free: The Art of Making Quality is Certain*, McGraw-Hill Book Company, New York, Mentor Printing : January 1980.

Crosby, Philip B., *Quality Without Tears: The Art of Hassle-Free Management*, McGraw-Hill Book Company, New York, Plume Printing, April 1985.

Logothetis, N., *Managing for Total Quality: From Deming to Taguchi and SPC*, Prentice Hall International (UK) Ltd. UK, 1992.

Joseph and Susan Berk, *Total Quality Management: Implementing Continuous Improvement*, Excel Books, India, 1995.

Hagan, Jack, *Management of Quality: Strategies to Improve Quality and the Bottom Line*, Oxford University Press, UK, 1997.

Davis, Elaine R., *Total Quality Management for Home Care"*, Aspen Publishers, Inc., USA, 1994.

Mondy, R. Wayne, *Management Concepts and Practices*, Allyn and Bacon Inc., USA, 1983.

Study Materials, *Notes on Total Quality Management*, National Institute of Information Technology [NIIT], India, 1997.

Study Materials, *Diploma in Business Administration*, National Council for Labour Management, Chennai: 1998.

2. Training

Martin, M. Broadwell, *The Supervisor and On-the-job Training*, Addison-Wesley Publishing Company, USA, 1995.

Belcourt, Monica Laura, *Managing Performance Through Training and Development*, Nelson, A Division of Thomson Learning, Canada : 2000.

Smith, Barry J., *How to Be an Effective Trainer*, John Wiley & Sons, Inc., USA, 1987.

3. Statistics and Scientific Knowledge

Park, K., *Park's Textbook of Preventive and Social Medicine*, M/s Banarsidas Bhanot Publishers, India: Fifteenth Edition, September 1997.

Blank, Leonard, *Changing Behavior in Individuals, Couples and Groups,* Charles C. Thomas Publishers Ltd., USA, 1996.

Kothari, C.R., *Research Methodology: Methods and Techniques*, Wiswa Prakashan, India, 1985.

Study Materials, *MA Sociology*, Annamalai University, India, 1997.

4. Computing Concepts

Study Materials, *Advanced Certificate in PC Application*, National Institute of Information Technology [NIIT], India, July 1997.

Study Materials, *Oracle Hand Book*, Software Solution Integrated Limited [SSI], Chennai, August 1998.

Study Materials, *Computing Concepts for Business [CSI 1301]*, Ottawa University, Canada, Fall 1999.

COMMENTS

I want to hear from you!!

By sharing your opinion about this book, you will help me to improve my writing. After reading this book, please provide me with answers to the following 10 questions.

1. Your profession
   - (i) Executive, Upper Management or Investor
   - (ii) Middle manager
   - (iii) Supervisor
   - (iv) Non-management Professionals
   - (v) Student

2. How did you come to know about this book?
   - (i) Advertisement
   - (ii) Training program
   - (iii) Friends
   - (iv) Display in book store

3. Your present country of residence
   ....

4. Concepts explained in this book
   - (i) Clearly explained
   - (ii) Need more explanation
   - (iii) Unclear

5. Illustrations and figures used in this book
    (i)   Very Effective
    (ii) Need more figures
    (iii) Ineffective

6. Examples given in this book
    (i)   Very useful
    (ii) Need more explanation
    (iii) Not useful

7. This book keeps your interest of reading
    (i)   Kept the interest constantly
    (ii) Need improvement
    (iii) Didn't keep me interested

8. After reading this book, your knowledge.
    (i)   Improved well
    (ii) Some improvement
    (iii) No improvement

9. After reading this book your opinion about profit and quality
    (i)   Quality is of prime importance
    (ii) Both Quality and Profit are important
    (iii) Profit is the most important

10. What do you like most about this book?

or

What do you not like about this book?

For contact information and info about other books written by Gana Kiritharan Please Visit:

www.gkiri.com

INDEX

usefulness of statistical
process service. (SPC), 81
Jidokha
meaning, 27
Juran, Dr Joseph. 3, 5-6
Just in time
meaning, 154

Kaizen
meaning, 27
Kamban system, 27
Kelvin, Lord, 65
Knowledge
classification, 167-169
lack and need of
improvement. 88-89

Lacocca, Lee, 8
Leadership, 116-117

MS Access, 197
example of DBMS, 189
MacArther
General Douglas. 4
Management and
administration difference,
28-29
concept, 16
functions, 117
quality. 117
MBWA (management by
walking around or
wandering about), 117
Management consultant
training, 131-132
Management literature
Dr Joseph Juran
contribution. 5
Management of Quality
by Dr Joseph Juran, 5
Manager
behave as counsellor and
friend, 118

problems, 102
professional training and
education, 119
quality management training,
11
understand employees goals
and needs, 104
Market
definition, 169
Maslows' Need Hierarchy
understanding employees'
goals and needs, 104-105
Mass Inspection or SPC
techniques, 22, 151-152
Measurement scales, 17
list, 73
others, 20
Mechanization
advantages and
disadvantages, 108
Middle Managers
responsibility, 143
training programme, 132
Money orientated quality
measurement scale, 20, 41
Motion picture technology
use for training and
demonstration in industry
and service, 129

New Technology
development, 120
Neiswanger, Prof. W.A., 160
Non-performance recording
checksheets, 74-75
control charts, 77-78
statistical process control,
80-81
Non-money orientated TQM
indices, 68
Normal distribution or normal
curve
concept, 182-183

SQL, 197-198
Surveillance system
introduction, 49
Slides
sizes, 129
Smith, Adam, 103, 107
Social Sciences
scientific method of
components, 159-164
Software
application, 188-189
categories, 187
compiler for programs, 188
MS-DOS, 187
pascal compiler for
program, 188
SUN operating system, 187
types, 188-189
UNIX function, 187
Windows Operating
System, 187
Specialization
increase in the production,
107
skills improvement, 107
US study, 107
Standard Deviation
concept, 183-184
steps, 184-185
Statistical Quality Control
(SQC) or Statistical
Process Control
technique, 22
Statistics
importance, 4
Stratified Random Sampling,
180
Structured Quarry Language
(SQL)
example of RDBMS, 192

Suggestion Form
to employess, 99-100
Suggestion system, 143, 150,
155
Supervisors, 116-117
responsibility, 143
training programe, 150
Sybase
example of RDBMS, 192
Systematic Random
Sampling, 179-180

Technicians
responsibility, 143
training programme, 132
Techniques or Tools
checksheets, 21-23
Fish Bone Diagram, 24-25
mass inspection, 22
Pareto chart, 24
statistical process control
(SPC), 22
variables, 23
Telephone of Bill
Laboratories example of
performance, 78
Textile Industry, England,
108
*The Art of Getting Your Own
Sweet Way* by Philip B.
Crosby, 6
Titanic experience, 40
Top management
responsibility, 142-143
Total Quality Management
(TQM)
concept, 3, 6-7, 16
Crosby's contribution, 6
definition, 6, 15-17

www.ingramcontent.com/pod-product-compliance
Lightning Source LLC
Chambersburg PA
CBHW031924190326
41519CB00007B/406